IS THE
HOLY LAND
HOLY?

IS THE
HOLY LAND HOLY?

LOUIS BAHJAT HAMADA, ph.D., Litt. D.

WINEPRESS WP PUBLISHING

ISBN 1-57921-143-7
Library of Congress Catalog Card Number: 98-61037

Other books by Louis Bahjat Hamada

God Loves the Arabs, Too

Understanding the Arab World

I dedicate this book to the One who came to this world not to condemn it "but that the world through Him might be saved" (John 3:17). Although He was spurned and vilified by unregenerate men and women, yet His unconditional love for the human race was manifest at the cross on Calvary. Such unspeakable love is incomprehensible (John 15:13).

ACKNOWLEDGMENTS

Unlike other authors who have had the good fortune of receiving adequate assistance in their scholarly research, I agonized painstakingly during the writing of this provocative and controversial book. The reason for that is I had to struggle much in my research to find the little known biblical and nonbiblical sources to substantiate the views presented in this timely volume. However, Dr. Walton Padelford was willing to engage with me in brainstorming and in typing the manuscript on his computer and word processor. He also helped me in some research. I am happy to render to him his dues (Rom. 13:7).

Moreover, I am indebted to my wife, Hanan, my helper, without whom my life would have been incomplete, unfruitful, and lonely (Gen. 2:18). God has blessed us with a son and a daughter.

Omar is a medical doctor and an ordained minister of the gospel of Christ. He is married to Tara Newton, who is also a medical doctor. The Lord has chosen her to be Omar's helper.

Sandra is a Christian clinical counselor. She is married to Dr. Andrew Combs, a chiropractor. God gave them a beautiful son, Nathan, who is being trained "in the way he should go" (Prov. 22:6). Hanan and I are claiming a quiver full of grandchildren (Ps 127:3–5; 128:1–4). My precious family has been an inspiration and encouragement to me.

I am also thankful to our prayer and financial supporters and to those who have consented to endorse my work on the back cover of this book. May our dear Lord and Savior, Jesus Christ, continue to bless their ministries richly. He promised to reward "those who diligently seek Him" (Heb. 11:6).

CONTENTS

PREFACE

O ne of my friends from the university had mentioned that I should get to know Dr. Louis Hamada because of his gift for Bible teaching and discipleship training. I tried, on one occasion, to attend a Bible class he was teaching for college students, but I was unable to make contact. Louis and I saw each other on a sporadic basis at church or in passing but never developed the depth of relationship that I desired until June 1982. While reading my Bible more or less at random, a passage in 3 John 5–8 came to my attention:

> Beloved, you do faithfully whatever you do for the brethren and for strangers, who have borne witness of your love before the church. If you send them forward on their journey in a manner worthy of God, you will do well, because they went forth for His name's sake, taking nothing from the Gentiles. We therefore ought to receive such, that we may become fellow workers for the truth.

Louis had taken a stand for godliness in the midst of trying circumstances and had lost his job of nine years. After receiving conflicting advice from many friends, he resolved to become an itinerant evangelist and Bible teacher. The Lord impressed me that day as I read 3 John that Louis was going out for the sake of Christ and that it would be well to help him on his journey. We talked that day, and plans were laid for the formation of The Hamada Evangelistic Outreach, Inc. Little did we know the far-reaching impact that afternoon's discussion would have on Arab evangelism.

Finances came along slowly, and a small, faith-ministry began. I remember hearing Louis pray for expanding opportunities to minister the Word of God. "Lord, use me or kill me" was the prayer that he would offer. Then we would marvel as new doors would open; but don't get the idea that hard physical work was not occurring. Many letters were written pursuing avenues for ministry. Sometimes as many as forty per week were sent out. This has led to a little, private joke between us when other pastors or Christian workers ask, "How do you get such unusual preaching opportunities?"

The answer is, "Brother, you must 'ask, seek, and knock'" (Matt. 7:7). Louis' tenacity and perseverance in the faith and the ministry have been an example and an encouragement to me.

Very soon after the formation of the ministry, Louis began to travel long distances in the US and overseas. In 1982, while on a Bible-teaching mission in Germany, he had an opportunity to travel to Israel for the purpose of making inroads evangelistically. While there, the Lord broke his heart over the condition of the Arab population in Israel. They were living as second-class citizens, discriminated against and dehumanized. After many years of preparation in Bible teaching, perseverance, and brokenness, the Lord gave him a burden for Arab evangelism. Afterward, the focus of the ministry shifted almost entirely toward it, whether in the form of one-on-one conversation with Arabs or of preaching in churches on God's blessings to Hagar and Ishmael for the purpose of encouraging the evangelical world to recognize the crying need of evangelizing Arabs and Muslims.

The Lord brought about this change of direction in ministry. Louis had every reason to avoid Arabs. He had been orphaned at a young age due to the political murder of his father and the ensuing suspicious death of his mother. He had been swindled out of his family inheritance in Lebanon and out of his life savings in Egypt. After so much harsh treatment, the natural reaction is to retaliate or to withdraw. Salvation cured the vengeance problem, and the trip to Israel changed the desire to withdraw from Arabs to a desire to minister to Arabs. The biblical studies and years of preparation were now focused on developing appropriate biblical teachings and apologetics to be used in Arab and Muslim evangelism. Louis and I rejoiced in new discoveries from Scripture that could further this task. At that point in 1984, he desired to write a book for the use of Christians and others that could answer questions and problems unique to the Arab or Muslim mind.

The trip to Israel had given him important ideas. A Palestinian man had stated that if it could be proven that God was not a Jew, he would believe in Jesus. The answer to this question may be known by some Christians, but Muslims have also heard of the doctrines of the Trinity and the Incarnation. We are claiming that Jesus of Nazareth is perfect God and perfect man, like the church fathers of old claimed. Logic would immediately lead us to note that since Jesus was a Jew and Jesus is God, then God must be a Jew. The subtle teaching of a racial God is a great stumbling stone to Muslims. Other controversies are just beneath the surface. What about the Son of God? Who are the chosen people of God? What if an Arab curses a Jew, would he be under the curse of God? These are emotional and controversial issues that must be tackled before we are effectively prepared to present the gospel to Muslims. So, the book began.

What an experience it was to work with Louis in a small way, doing research and reading manuscripts. I would come to his house in the afternoon, where he was writing at his kitchen table, hair disheveled, Arabic coffee at his hand, and ancient volumes piled high. The process of doing biblical and historical research is time consuming yet exhilarating. Dusty, out-of-print volumes might not seem to offer much to the average reader, but gems of truth are found there that the author uses to build his case. For instance, Louis had believed for years that the Arabic phrase *beni-Kahtan* (sons of Kahtan) referred to the biblical Joktan of Genesis 10:25–29, the progenitor of the original thirteen Arabian tribes. This belief was confirmed through historical research, and the story of Joktan became an important link in tracing the lineage of the Arabs.

Remarkable also was the fact that Louis did not have a publisher, due to the controversial nature of the theological studies contained in the work. This venture in writing has been abundantly blessed. Within a year, the book was finished. *God Loves the Arabs, Too* was published and circulated all over the world. Louis still gets calls and letters from people who have read this book. Louis dealt with difficult theological and apologetic matters, such as understanding salvation history, end-time prophecy, and the doctrine of the blood of Christ and the blood of Adam. It should be a classic in schools of mission throughout the evangelical world.

Preaching and teaching missions followed. In Europe, opportunities opened in Italy, Germany, England, Belgium, France, the Netherlands, and Austria. In the US and Canada, preaching dates came from churches too numerous to mention. In the Middle East, ministry opportunities opened in Lebanon, Israel, the United Arab Emirates, and Oman. In Asia, South America, and other parts of the world, seminary teaching and training of young people interested in missions to Muslims ensued. No doubt the Lord Himself is doing these things. I remember meeting a young man from Lebanon who had believed in Messiah Jesus after attending a series of meetings conducted by Dr. Hamada. The patient research and teaching ministry were paying off. Muslims were turning to Christ. Clearly, a cultural and evangelistic key had been found that could open the hearts of many to Christ.

A second book was written, *Understanding the Arab World*, which enumerated the good and great contributions of Arab culture to world civilization and illustrated God's unconditional love for Arabs. It also encouraged Christians to understand the Middle Eastern situation and mindset—in other words, to walk a mile in another man's moccasins. Thomas Nelson agreed to publish his book, and this has also opened many doors for him and his lovely wife, Hanan, to speak before groups and to have personal conversation with interested Arabs. The answering machine regularly reports new telephone numbers of Arab friends desiring to talk about spiritual life in general or Messiah in particular.

There is a problem of understanding in evangelical and fundamentalist circles today. The problem is that the modern state of Israel is zealously and uncritically held in too high a place of esteem. The reasons for this are, no doubt, varied and complex, but the primary reason stems from premillennial eschatology, which we certainly do not reject. However, in some circles an unbalanced absorption in the Second Coming of Christ has led us to forget the first coming of Christ—i.e., that Israel needs to be evangelized worse than she needs financial aid or arms. The active evangelization of modern Israel and the Arab world is the mandate that our Savior gave us:

> All authority has been given to Me in heaven and on earth. Go therefore and make disciples of all the nations, baptizing them in the name of the Father and of the Son and of the Holy Spirit, teaching them to observe all things that I have commanded you; and lo, I am with you always, even to the end of the age. (Matt. 28:18–20)

> My kingdom is not of this world. (John 18:36)

We are wasting our energy in a vain attempt to manipulate the kingdoms of this world into the shape we think they should have. Our prayer, energy, and sweat should be expended in our basic task of preaching the gospel to all people, including Arabs and Jews.

This problem sets the stage for Dr. Hamada's third book, *Is the Holy Land Holy?* How does the Bible deal with Arabs? What promises do they have? How has God used them historically and prophetically to fulfill His purpose? These are some of the important questions that need to be answered. Again, Louis is trying to accomplish two goals: edifying the body of Christ, and showing Christ's love to those who do not currently confess Him as their Messiah. God does not play favorites. The door to intimate communion with the Father is open to all who will "kiss the Son" (Ps. 2:12).

WALTON M. PADELFORD, Ph.D.
Professor of Economics, Union University
Jackson, Tennessee

FOREWORD

O ne of the great and ironic tragedies of human history is
the incessant and brutal war that has been waged in the
name of religion. And this is not limited to the fringe groups
or nonmonotheistic faiths, for the three great religions that
confess a belief in only one God—Judaism, Christianity, and
Islam—have been at the forefront of such conflict for a millennium and a half. To compound the irony, all three promote peace as the ideal in both their sacred writings and
their public pronouncements.

It is important to distinguish the inspired or official doctrine of a religious tradition from the actual practice of its
adherents. There is frequently (or usually) a wide divergence
between what religious people profess as tenets of their faith
and what they carry out in everyday corporate and personal
life. Christians are especially quick to point out the difference between true faith, which is the faith of the regenerate,
and the superficial lip service paid to biblical revelation by
those who know nothing of redeeming grace. It might be
surprising to know that all high religions make such distinctions and attribute the wicked behavior of some of their devotees as reflective of extremists or of those who remain unen-
lightened to true faith.

It is against this background that Louis Hamada develops much of his thought and argumentation in his *Is the Holy*

Land Holy? As an Arab Christian, he helps to redress the often biased, one-sided view that exonerates Israel vis-á-vis the Arabs and Islam and Christians in their dealings with both Jews and Arabs, especially in the Crusades. His careful research documents the fact that all three religions have bloody hands as a result of their centuries of misunderstanding and mistreating one another.

More positively, Dr. Hamada focuses on the redemptive grace of God in Christ, which has made all humankind one by common faith. Jew, Gentile, Arab are all objects of His love, and in response to that love, enter into one body—a fellowship that transcends the distinctions of race, culture, class, and ideology. But Hamada's concern that mutual suspicions and uneradicated prejudices remain is well placed, for all sensitive observers of the contemporary scene are aware of the insidious nature of the religious and political polarization, which exists even in close-knit and genuine Christian communities. It is his plea here that these divisive tendencies be surrendered to the God of peace, who wishes nothing more than that His children celebrate their oneness and put aside an unbiblical predilection toward factionalism. Would that his plea be heeded so that together redeemed Jews, Gentiles, and Arabs of the earth might give expression to God's eternal purpose of reconciling the world to Himself.

EUGENE H. MERRILL, Ph.D.
Professor of Old Testament Studies
Dallas Theological Seminary
Dallas, Texas

One

UNHOLY ALLIANCE

I was invited by the president of The Religious Roundtable to participate in The Twelfth Annual International Christian Prayer Breakfast meeting to pray for the peace of Jerusalem. The meeting took place on October 15, 1993, at the Peabody Hotel in Memphis, Tennessee. More than one-thousand guests attended. Most of them came from across America, but some of them were flown from Israel.

Speaker after speaker reviewed in minute detail how six million Jews were killed in Nazi Germany and how God has blessed America over the years for standing with Israel politically and financially.

Although I recoil at the horrors of the Holocaust, the speeches dumbfounded me. The prayer breakfast had turned into a prolonged outburst of bitter memories of past persecutions of the Jews. Then a prominent pastor of a large Baptist church gave a powerful sermon in favor of Israel's political and financial support, but practically nothing was said about how to have peace with God through our Lord Jesus Christ (Rom. 5:1).

Another notable speaker emphasized the belief that Israel needs America's financial and political support and that Palestine belongs to the Jewish people. Eventually, a long proclamation of blessing was read as follows:

> As Bible-believing Americans, . . . we support Israel's right to their land spiritually and legally. History records that

God deals with nations in accordance with how these nations deal with Israel. . . . We consider the support of Israel a biblical mandate. . . .

The basis for this proclamation was Genesis 12:3:

I will bless those who bless you, and I will curse him who curses you; and in you all the families of the earth shall be blessed.

The foregoing proclamation of blessing is based on a misinterpretation of Scripture. What remains peculiar about that interpretation is that there is more emphasis on Israel than on the birth, death, and bodily resurrection of the Lord Jesus Christ as the fulfillment of this prophecy. That misconstrued interpretation of Genesis 12:3 has caused much harm to the message of Christ and has promoted a racial and political theology. Ironically, Christian Zionists consider that passage to be the foundation of the covenant relationship between God and Israel and for their belief in Israel's sacredness. They claim that God will deal with the nations in relation to how they treat Israel.[1]

Zionism Is Not Judaism

Political Zionism started in Europe approximately one hundred years ago under the impact of anti-Semitism. An Austrian journalist by the name of Theodore Herzl went to Paris in 1896 to report the Dreyfus case for a Viennese newspaper. The *Dreyfus* case occupied Europe for a long time due to its controversial nature.

Dreyfus was a Jew and a respected high-ranking officer in the French army. Europe had anti-Semitic sentiments during that time. Dreyfus was used as a scapegoat and was falsely accused of collaborating with the Germans against France. Without finding any incriminating evidence against him, the court sentenced him to lifelong exile.

The Dreyfus case coupled with anti-Semitic feelings toward the Jews gave Herzl the impetus to write *Der Judenstaat* (The Jewish State). In 1897 he organized and presided over the first Zionist congress in Basel, Switzerland. Political Zionism was born at that time with a burning desire to return to Zion at all costs. Herzl and his counterparts were convinced that political Zionism was the only answer for overcoming anti-Semitism. After much deliberation, this newly formed organization adopted an almost holy-war strategy to establish a national home for the dispersed Jews.

At the turn of the twentieth century neither the Arabs nor the European Zionists were belligerent toward each other. However, the Allies (the British and the French) had adopted pro-Jewish attitudes as a result of Christian-Zionist theological persuasion from evangelical circles during the nineteenth century. The Allies decided it was to their advantage politically and economically to exploit this historical event of the Jews' return to Palestine. They were aware of the fact that the Turks had outlived their usefulness in the Middle East. The Allies had wanted to end the Turkish subjection of the Arabs since 1516—especially now since the Turks were allied with Germany and Austria during World War I.[2]

With the help of Lawrence of Arabia, a British agent serving in the Middle East, the Allies were able to woo key Arab leaders and persuade them to fight against the Turks in order to uproot them from their lands. In return, the British made some promises they did not intend to keep. They promised Emir Faisal (king of Iraq in 1920) a postwar independent Arab state. Those promises were made to Sharif Hussein of Mecca by Sir Henry McMahon, the British high commissioner in Egypt.

In 1917 the British also made promises to the Zionist organization to the effect that Palestine would become an independent Jewish national home. This was known as the Balfour Declaration, the famous letter from Lord Balfour sent to the British Zionist chemist, Chaim Weizmann. This kind of subtle political maneuvering overturned the idea of peaceful coexistence between Arabs and Jews and set the Middle East on a course of hostility and bloody wars. I believe, along with many others, that the conflict between Arabs and Jews has already reached a point of no return.[3]

Ironically, the leading men and women in Zionism have long rejected categorically the divine origin of the Bible, thereby reducing the five books of Moses and the writings of the prophets of the Old Testament to mere folklore and ancient tales. Nevertheless, the proponents of political Zionism often appeal to scriptural references relating to Israel in order to justify their systematic political maneuvering.

The aim of Zionism has been to uproot the Palestinians from their homeland, by pursuing a calculated course of usurpation and to encourage Jews in countries throughout the world to return to the state of Israel in order to build a mighty militaristic country. Zionism has invested great sums of money for propaganda purposes and has been successful in persuading many countries to join its coalitions and alliances.

The average sympathizers with Zionism are, more often than not, innocent and well-meaning individuals who honestly believe in the Bible or who believe that they are engaged in humanitarian or charitable work or that they are participating in a worthy endeavor of national revival of Israel.

History is repeating itself. The Jews became a nation in the wilderness and were misled by false prophets and worshipped the golden calf. They have followed false messianic movements throughout their history down to today's Zionism. The prophet Daniel predicted that such deceptions would continue to be fulfilled in Israel until the Lord Jesus Himself delivers a remnant of the Jews from a time of trouble such as never was since there was a nation: "[Then they] shall be delivered, Every one who is found written in the book" (Dan. 12:1).

Unlike Zionism, ancient Judaism is entirely different because it was initiated by God Himself. The Jews were chosen to be God's peculiar people. They were chosen to make Him known to the whole world through the Torah and the writings of the Hebrew prophets. These writings point toward the coming to earth of the Holy One of Israel, the sin-bearing Messiah. It is for this reason that Paul says that to them were committed the oracles of God (Rom. 3:2).

24

It needs to be understood that certain wars and killings were sanctioned by God Himself in the Old Testament for certain reasons, but the New Testament teaching forbids killing and other inhumane acts. The Lord Jesus clarified this truth in the Sermon on the Mount (Matt. 5–7). The biblically oriented Jew should be opposed to the expulsion of the Palestinians from their legal right to their homeland, because they are included in God's prophetic plan.

> A mixed race shall settle in Ashdod [one of the five Palestinian cities; see Joshua 13:3], and I will cut off the pride of the Philistines. I will take away the blood from his mouth, and the abominations from between his teeth. But he who remains, even he shall be for our God, and shall be like a leader in Judah. (Zech. 9:6–7).

The prophet Zechariah predicted that a remnant of the Palestinians (Philistines) will be cleansed from false worship and converted to the Messiah. This remnant will then occupy a place of leadership or possibly be like a family within Judah.

The Alliance

Israeli officials and American Jewish leaders have compromised their religious beliefs in exchange for what is perceived as support from influential Christian fundamentalists.[4] Although the Zionist Jews neither believe in the deity of Christ, nor do they allow Christians to evangelize in the nation of Israel,[5] former Prime Minister Menachem Begin and the Likud government have supported such an alliance to gain American financial and political support.[6]

The late Mr. Begin proudly claimed a personal friendship with noted televangelists. According to a Nielsen survey, more than sixty million listeners hear teaching and preaching regularly concerning the chosen people of God and a chosen land. The Israeli victory in the summer of 1967 and the subsequent occupation of the West Bank, Gaza Strip, and the Golan Heights were hailed by many Christians as a thrill and a source of renewed faith in the promises God made to Israel.[7]

The televangelists of the evangelical right wing have already left their mark on local, national, and international US policy. They have convinced their listeners that Israel reigns supreme in God's eyes and that the fate of other nations lies in their attitude toward Israel. This cult of Israel is known as Christian Zionism. Zionists believe God has promised Israel exclusive possession of the Promised Land and that He will act in their behalf to fulfill the promise.

God's purpose in the Old Testament for delivering Israel from Egyptian bondage was to establish them as a kingdom of priests and a holy nation (Exod. 19:6 and Deut. 26:19). As priests, or typical mediators between God and man, the biblical Hebrews were to be the vessels by which God's knowledge would overflow to the nations. God wanted to be the King of His chosen people so He might protect them from their enemies and use them as His witnesses. The ancient Hebrews had an exclusive assignment to be a blessing by witnessing to the world of the goodness and faithfulness of God, as Isaiah understood:

> You are my witnesses, says the Lord, And My servant whom I have chosen.... And understand that I am He. Before Me there was no God formed, Nor shall there be after Me. I, even I, am the Lord, And besides Me there is no savior.... Therefore you are My witnesses, says the Lord, that I am God. (Isa. 43:10–12)

God wanted to appoint the Hebrews as His ambassadors so the whole world might know that God is the only Lord and Savior of humanity. For this reason, God sent the prophet Samuel to deliver His wishes to the people. When Samuel shared with the people what God said, the Hebrews rejected God's demand and requested instead a human king, to rule them and to judge them like all the nations (1 Sam. 8:5).

Their foolish decision grieved Samuel. The prophet reported to the Lord that the people would like to have a monarchy in place of a theocracy. In reply, God said to Samuel:

Heed the voice of the people in all that they say to you; for they have not rejected you, but they have rejected Me, that I should not reign over them. According to all the works which they have done since the day that I brought them up out of Egypt, even to this day with which they have forsaken Me and served other gods. . . . Now therefore, heed their voice. However, you shall solemnly forewarn them, and show them the behavior of the king who will reign over them. (1 Sam. 8:7)

That was a sad day for the Hebrews when they rejected God's demand. "He gave them their request, but sent leanness into their soul" (Ps. 106:15). Samuel conveyed to them many additional warnings for their stubborn and rebellious attitude and predicted a fearful future for them if they continued to live according to their desires.

Sadly, from that moment on, most Jews have not kept God's commandments, and they have steadily acted contrary to His wishes. By doing what was right in [their] own eyes (Judg. 21:25), Israel ceased to be a holy nation with a special calling and purpose (see Deut. 28). Their rebellious attitude was just another outgrowth of the Garden rebellion (Gen. 3).

Even when the Messiah came to save Israel from the penalty of their sin, they did not receive Him (John 1:11). They rejected Him and refused to accept His claims as having divine authority over sin and death. Not only that, but they requested that He should be put to death, by saying:

Let Him be crucified. . . . His blood be on us and on our children. (Matt. 27:22–25)

As a result of their willful refusal to believe in the Messiah as their Lord and Savior, the Lord Jesus rebuked the religious leaders of Israel and said to them:

The Kingdom of God will be taken from you and given to a nation bearing the fruits of it (Matt. 21:43; cf. 8:12).

Today the chosen people with a special calling and purpose are the universal community of believers in the Messiah. God has always accepted people, whether they are Jews or Gentiles, into fellowship with Himself on the basis of grace through faith (Eph. 2:4–10). Therefore, God's chosen people are those who are

> led by the Spirit of God, these are sons of God . . . the Israel of God. . . . He chose [them] in Him [Jesus Christ] before the foundation of the world. . . . [They] are a chosen generation, a royal priesthood, a holy nation, His own special people, that [they] may proclaim the praises of Him who called [them] out of darkness into His marvelous light (Rom. 8:14–16; Gal. 6:16; Eph. 1:4–6; 1 Pet. 2:9).

In disobedience, Israel represents all other religious groups who have corporately and individually disobeyed God. Stephen summarized the foregoing, by saying:

> You stiff-necked and uncircumcised in heart and ears! You always resist the Holy Spirit; as your fathers did, so do you. Which of the prophets did your fathers not persecute? And they killed those who foretold the coming of the Just One [Jesus Christ], of whom you now have become the betrayers and murderers, who have received the law by the direction of angels and have not kept it (Acts 7:51–53; cf. Luke 11:46–52).

The prophets of the Old Testament along with the writers of the New Testament reserved their harshest criticism for the people of Israel, chiefly because to them were committed the oracles of God (Rom. 3:2). God chose the Jews to be His witnesses, and no other people have witnessed God's presence as have the Jews. Yet, most of them are still living in unbelief.

However, the Israeli government has encouraged some Christian leaders to keep on preaching and teaching any biblical theme that serves as a propaganda vehicle for Israel's benefit. There are several Christian groups in Israel who are trying to propagate the idea that God will judge nations that bring harm on the chosen people of God.

The Meaning of Genesis 12:3

Paul unlocked Genesis 12:3 by his statement in Galatians 3:7: "Therefore know that only those who are of faith are sons of Abraham." Paul was saying to Galatian Christians tempted to return to the ways of Judaism that it is not Abraham's natural descendants, but his spiritual ones who are his true children. The word *therefore* points the reader back to the preceding verses. In verse 6 Paul appealed to Genesis 15:6, and in verse 5 he declared that it was by faith that the Holy Spirit had been received by Abraham, and that was indisputable evidence of sonship (Rom. 8:14).

Romans 4:11 asserts that Abraham is the father of all those who believe, though they are uncircumcised, that righteousness might be imputed [transferred] to them also. Abraham was the first to participate in the rite of circumcision in order to confirm his faith. Salvation occurred *before* the law was given and the rite of circumcision had been established; salvation was not by faith *plus* keeping the law, but justification was, and still is, by faith alone (Rom. 4:9–25).

The promise God made to Abraham in Genesis 12:3 is a favor, not to be earned or merited by good works. Paul made it very clear that the seed that will inherit the blessing is not to be equated with those who live under the law, but rather those who share Abraham's faith (Rom. 4:16).

The doctrine of justification by faith alone was so abhorrent to the Jews because they could not understand why God should forgive the guilty, let alone justify them by faith. For this and other reasons, they rejected Jesus as the Messiah and utterly disregarded his redemptive plan. However, the doctrine of justification by faith was not something new. The Old Testament confirms that God credits righteousness to those who put their trust in Him by faith, and the New Testament shows more clearly that salvation is received by faith (Ps. 37:39; cf. Phil. 3:9).

Paul used Abraham as an example to show that the promise of Genesis 12:3 did embody the principles of being declared righteous by believing and trusting God for salvation. Therefore, Abraham's faith was credited to him for righteousness (Gen. 15:6; cf. Rom. 4:3). In like manner, Peter quoted Genesis 12:3: "And in your seed all the families of the earth shall be blessed" (Acts 3:25). Peter's words *in your seed* had all nations in mind and held up Abraham as an example of faith—a faith available to anyone who believes in Jesus Christ.

The misinterpretation of Genesis 12:3 has impeded missionary work among more than 1.5 billion Arabs and Muslims. Did God say that He would bless those who bless the physical Israel and curse those who curse the Jews? Of course not! Neither did He promise to bless or curse those who are kind or unkind to the Jews. The New Testament applies Genesis 12:3 to Christ and His spiritual seed (1 John 3:9; cf. Gal. 3:14). Paul argued in Romans 2:28–29 that the true Jew is one who has been circumcised spiritually; being Abraham's physical seed does not give all his descendants the right to be called children of God. Abraham's blessing is passed on only to those who have a like faith, for Paul wrote that "those who are of faith are blessed with believing Abraham" (Gal. 3:9). On the other hand, all unbelieving Jews and Gentiles are under the curse of God (John 3:36).

God chose Abraham in order that He might bless believers with eternal salvation through the atoning death of the Lord Jesus (Rev. 5:9). Under the same provision all unregenerate Jews and Gentiles are cursed with eternal condemnation (John 5:21–25). The promise of Genesis 12:3—"And in you all the families of the earth shall be blessed,"—is amplified by Genesis 22:18 and repeated in Acts 3:25, which states, "In your seed all the nations of the earth shall be blessed." This promise was made "till the Seed should come" (Gal. 3:19), referring expressly to Abraham's need of a physical heir through whom the promise of the blessing (salvation) and of the curse (condemnation) should be fulfilled.

The blessing and cursing by God in Genesis 12:3 apply only to salvation and damnation. We see that the seed mentioned here is the Lord Jesus and none other (Gal. 3:16).

Since Abraham is a key figure in the teaching of the three monotheistic religions, it is imperative at this juncture to shed some light on his origin. Most western Christians and others would be surprised to learn that Abraham and Sarah were not Jews. The word Jew, *Yehudi* in the Hebrew, refers to those descended from Judah, one of the twelve sons of Jacob (Gen. 29:35). Abraham was the first person to be called the *Hebrew* (Gen. 14:13), meaning "one from the other side." The term designated at that time an ethnic people who lived a nomadic life like Abraham. It may also have some connection to his origin since the Canaanites considered him a migrant from Ur (modern Iraq) and Haran, a Southwestern district of Syria.

Abraham, Sarah, and all their relatives were not Jews; they were Gentile pagans from Mesopotamia (Acts 7:2), who served other gods (Josh. 24:2). The Jews were called Hebrews because they descended from Eber (Gen. 11:16–26). William Whiston, who translated the complete works of Flavius Josephus, stated:

> The Jews were called Hebrews, from this their progenitor Heber, our author Josephus here rightly affirms; and not from Abram the Hebrew, or passenger over Euphrates, as many of the moderns suppose. Shem is also called the father of all the children of Heber, or of all the Hebrews, in a history long before Abram passed over Euphrates (Gen. xiv. 13) where the original says they told Abram the Hebrew, the Septuagint renders it the passenger. But this is spoken only of Abram himself, who had then lately passed over Euphrates: and is another signification of the Hebrew word, taken as an appellative, and not as a proper name.[8]

The Gospel Given to Abraham

How did God preach the gospel of Christ to Abraham? Once more Paul has explained another controversial spiritual mystery:

And the Scripture, foreseeing that God would justify the Gentiles by faith, preached the gospel to Abraham beforehand, saying, In you all the nations shall be blessed. (Gal. 3:8)

Genesis 3:15 hints at the Redeemer's virgin birth two thousand years later. God called Abraham to make him the means by which this prediction could be fulfilled (Gen. 22:18). Similarly, Acts 7:2 explains:

And he said, "Brethren and fathers, listen: The God of glory appeared to our father Abraham when he was in Mesopotamia, before he dwelt in Haran."

God appeared to Abraham in Ur and saved him because God had decided to bless all the nations of the earth through the incarnation of the Messiah so that He might save sinners (1 Tim. 1:15), rescuing them from the wrath to come (Matt. 3:7). Evidently God preached the gospel of Christ to Abraham and revealed to him the mystery of godliness (1 Tim. 3:16), which is Christ's incarnation, death, burial, resurrection, and ascension into heaven (2 Tim. 1:10; cf. Acts 1:9–11; 1 Cor. 15:1–6).

Paul attests to the fact that salvation can be received only by grace through faith, and faith involves knowledge of the gospel of Christ, and knowledge includes acceptance of and adherence to the truth of the gospel (Eph. 2:8; cf. Rom. 10:14). Therefore, since faith comes by hearing, and hearing by the word of God (Rom. 10:17), Abraham must have heard the gospel from God Himself (Gal. 3:8).

Subsequently, Abraham understood that God would not kill Isaac and that Isaac was a picture-prophecy concerning the death of the only begotten Son of God (Gen. 22:8; cf. Heb. 11:17–19). The idea of the ram being offered as a substitute for Isaac originated with God in order to illustrate the substitutionary sacrifice of the Lamb of God (John 1:29). The substitutionary sacrifice of Genesis 22 is linked metaphorically to the Passover lamb of Exodus 12:11, a breathtaking picture of the finished redemptive work of Christ at Calvary (1 Cor. 5:7)!

Esau, Jacob, and Genesis 12:3

Since God changed Jacob's name to Israel, many have been conditioned to believe that God repeated Genesis 12:3 to Jacob, thereby cursing those who curse Israel and blessing those who bless Israel in the following words from Genesis 27:29:

> Cursed be everyone who curses you, And blessed be those who bless you.

God did not say that, but Isaac did. However, it is difficult to understand how the crafty Rebekah was able to teach her favorite son, Jacob, to lie to his blind father concerning his true identity and to resort to trickery in order to receive the blessing of the firstborn (Gen. 27:1–29).

It is true that Esau was a "profane person . . . who for one morsel of food sold his birthright . . . that afterward, when he wanted to inherit the blessing, he was rejected. . . ." (Heb. 12:16–17). Nevertheless, Rebekah

> could not risk waiting for God to work out his plans in his own way. So she resorted to the most contemptible deceit to secure the blessing for her younger son. . . . Coached by his mother, Jacob came before his old father with deception and lies. He even declared that Jehovah had helped him make his preparation with speed. After lying to his father, he planted a false kiss upon the old man's upturned face.[9]

The great tragedy for Esau, Isaac's favorite son (see Gen. 27), was that he did not know that his own mother and brother would conspire against him. What agony and disappointment Esau must have felt when he discovered that his younger brother had secured the blessing through trickery. Thereafter, Esau's heart became hardened and his hatred toward his brother was kindled.

Many televangelists and their counterparts have been trying relentlessly to justify Israel's usurpation of the Promised Land from the Palestinians by appealing to Genesis 12:3

and other misinterpreted verses. Their theological persuasion springs from an ill-conceived hermeneutical procedure, mainly because there is a misunderstanding of the apostolic method of Old Testament interpretation, which finds Christ to be the focal point. In other words, the great salvation themes of the death and resurrection of Christ are contained throughout the Old Testament. He is the key to understanding the entire Bible as taught in the Law of Moses, the Psalms, and the Prophets, or as the Hebrews say, "the Tanach."

> And beginning at Moses and all the prophets, He expounded to them in all the Scriptures the things concerning Himself. (Luke 24:27)

This promulgation of evangelists and other advocates of Israel has accomplished at least three things: (1) the once oppressed Jews have been successful in gaining financial and political support from the American taxpayers; (2) millions of Christians have been conditioned to believe that God is blessing America for helping God's chosen people in every possible way; and (3) most Arabs and Muslims have hardened their hearts against the Jews, and against "the light of the gospel of the glory of Christ" (2 Cor. 4:4).

Misinterpretation from the Talmud

The *Talmud*, meaning "instruction," is a detailed compilation of Oral Law of the Jews with prolonged rabbinical elaborations and commentaries in contradistinction to the holy Scriptures. It is comprised of two divisions, which are the Mishna (the Hebrew text of the Oral Law) and the Gemara (the Aramaic commentary on the Mishna). The Mishna and Gemara together became known as the Talmud. The Talmud is the authoritative collection of rabbinic law, supposed by Orthodox Jews to have been given by God Himself to Moses on Mount Sinai. Based on their belief, these laws were handed down orally from Moses and passed on from generation to generation to the time of Christ.

Origin of the Talmud

There are two Talmuds that were written by the Rabbis—one in Palestine and the other in Babylonia. Both the Palestinian and Babylonian Talmuds were compiled between the fifth and sixth centuries A.D. However, the Babylonian Talmud is viewed by Orthodox Jews as the most authoritative version. The Babylonian Talmud in its complete form is available in English in various editions. The Talmud is arranged in six Orders (Sedarim), each of which contains books called Tractates (Massekoth). Each tractate is numbered with double pages. The first is called *a*, the second *b*.

Orthodox Jews maintain that the Talmud is the most authoritative and true exposition of Scripture, having been dictated by God Himself. They assert that the New Testament is false and misleading while the Talmud is pure and holy. Not only that, the Talmud teaches that our Lord Jesus is a bastard and that Mary was a harlot.[10] Sometimes, He is referred to under the name of Balaam, the son of Behor.

> It is clear, therefore, that the Jewish legends deny the resurrection of Jesus; the halakic assertion that Balaam (i.e. the prototype of Jesus) had no part in the future life must also be especially noted (Sanh. x. 2).

> It is further said: "The pupils of the recreant Balaam inherit hell" (Abot. v. 19).[11]

The Role of Pharisees in the Talmud

Orthodox Jews seem to revere the opinions of the Pharisees, as contained in the Talmud, more than the Torah (the five books of Moses). During the Babylonian captivity, the Jews were deprived of their cherished Temple and other ritualistic practices. A class of teachers called the scribes (sopherim) concocted new laws and regulations that made possible the revival of the Jewish religion. This system of interpretation appears to have been harmless in the beginning, but the scribes began to contradict the Old Testament. Thus a new method of interpretation had evolved in order to allow the scribes to exegete the Torah beyond its literal meaning. When the Torah was opposed to the interpretation of the scribes, they

> attempted whenever possible not to abolish it, but to introduce some legal fiction whereby the authority of the law was upheld and yet at the same time rendered null and void for all practical purposes.[12]

The Pharisee, following the scribal tradition, interpreted the Old Testament according to its ceremonial purity.

> For this reason, they could not purchase items of food or drink from a sinner for fear of ceremonial defilement. Nor could a Pharisee eat in the house of a sinner. . . . Pharisaic thought, began as a commentary on the Law, but it was ultimately raised to the level of Law itself. To justify this teaching, it was maintained that the oral law was given by God to Moses on Mount Sinai along with the written law or Torah. (Pirke Aboth, 1:1)

> The ultimate in this development is reached when the Mishna states that oral law must be observed with greater stringency than the written law, because statutory law (that is, oral tradition) affects the life of the ordinary man more intimately than the more remote constitutional law. (M. Sanhedrin, 10:3)

The Pharisees contend that they had the key to interpreting the Scriptures. The Talmud teaches that Moses ascended to heaven and heard Rabbi Akiba (still unborn) explaining the Torah in an astonishing manner (Menachoth 29*b*). The Rabbis (Pharisees) believe that they are the possessors of the Oral Law, which was handed down from Moses.

> Moses received the Torah at Sinai and transmitted it to Joshua, Joshua to the Elders, and the Elders to the Prophets, and the Prophets to the men of the Great Synagogue.

Scripture and its complementary Oral Instruction, with special reference to the latter.
Joshua received from Moses. The transmission and reception were done orally.[13]

The word *Pharisee* means "separated one." The Pharisees could be traced to the Maccabean times when orthodox Jews separated themselves from the corrupting influence of Hellenistic (Greek) immoral and occultic practices. They maintained their separation from defilement, but not from the Jewish community itself, while the Pharisee might hold himself aloof from sinners, he lived among them and coveted their esteem.

The Pharisees claimed that they could overturn anything Moses had said if it contradicted their teachings. When a Rabbi has been publicly recognized by his fellow Pharisees as a prominent person, then

> he is, by virtue of his position as chief of the court of justice, invested with the same authority as Moses (Sifre, Deut. 153; R.H. 25*ab*). Even when they decide that left should be right, or right left, when they are mistaken or misled in their judgment, they must be obeyed.[14]

The Talmud teaches that the prophetic gift was taken from the prophets of God and given to the sages (wise men). *The Jewish Encyclopedia* tells us that we must turn to the "genius" of the Jews and their leaders in order to understand the secret of its (Judaism's) power.

> It has grown out of the soul of the Jewish people. . . .
> Whereas Buddhism centers in the Buddha and Christianity in the Christ, Judaism centers in no one personality.[15]

To say it differently, the religious life of Israel no longer consisted in the belief and obedience of the inspired revelation of the Old Testament, but Judaism became the religion of Israel, where the Jewish people were "the center of gravity."[16]

The Results in Modern Judaism

Modern Judaism has been greatly influenced by the teachings of the Talmud:

> The Jewish religion as it is today traces its descent without a break through all the centuries from the pharisees. Their leading ideas and methods found expression in a literature of enormous extent, of which a very great deal is still in existence. The Talmud is the largest and most important single piece of that literature . . . and the study of it is essential for any real understanding of Pharisaism.[17]

Modern Israel still considers the Talmud to be its highest religious authority. Michael L. Rodkinson in the editor's preface to the New Edition of the Babylonian Talmud states, "The modern Jew is the product of the Talmud." Louis Finkelstein, Professor of Theology at Jewish Theological Seminary of America, came to the conclusion that Pharisaism became Talmudism, which became medieval Rabbinism, which became modern Rabbinism. This historical persistance illustrates the "unique and astonishing durability of Pharisaism."[18]

Jesus and the Pharisees

Many Jews and Christian Zionists say that Christ's statement to the Pharisees in John 8:44 that their "father [was] the devil," is anti-Semitic and should therefore be removed from the Bible. Some contend that the Lord Jesus never said these words but that they were attributed to Him by those who opposed the Pharisees.

After the destruction of the Temple, the religious life of Israel was reconstructed and regulated

> from the pharisaic point of view. . . . Pharisaism shaped the character of Judaism and the life and thought of the Jew for all of the future."[19]

The seed of Talmudic teaching was planted during the Babylonian exile. It was called "oral tradition" and consisted of hairsplitting arguments and elaborations on rabbinical interpretation of the Law of Moses (Midrashim), and the new pharisaic laws (Halaka).

Subsequently, oral tradition became known during the time of our Lord as "Tradition of the Elders." Those traditions were the framework of the written Talmud and other rabbinic tales and legends comprising "a body of 613 rules designed to regulate every aspect of life."[20]

One of the traditions was the washing of hands before eating (Mark 7:4). When the Pharisees and Scribes asked the Lord Jesus, "Why do your disciples not walk according to the tradition of the elders. . . ." He answered and said to them,

> Well did Isaiah prophesy of you hypocrites. . . . You hold the tradition of men—the washing of pitchers and cups, and many other such things you do. . . . You reject the commandment of God, that you may keep your tradition. . . . making the word of God of no effect through your tradition that you have handed down. (Mark 7:5–13)

The Pharisees and Scribes followed the Lord Jesus from place to place to undermine His authority by criticizing Him and His disciples publicly for not obeying their tradition. These attitudes have developed into accepted Jewish views of Jesus. *The Jewish Encyclopedia* article on Jesus, reveals some Judaic views of Jesus:

> It is the tendency of all these sources to belittle the person of Jesus by ascribing to him illegitimate birth, magic, and a shameful death. . . . All of the Toledot editions [medieval rabbinic tales about the acts of the Lord Jesus] contain a story of a dispute which Jesus carried on with the scribes, who on the ground of that dispute declared him to be a bastard.[21]

The Talmud says:

> On the eve of the Passover Yeshu [the Nazarean] was hanged. For forty days before the execution took place a herald went forth and cried, "He is going forth to be stoned

because he has practiced sorcery and enticed Israel to apostasy. Anyone who can say anything in his favour, let him come forward and plead on his behalf." But since nothing was brought forward in his favour he was hanged on the eve of the Passover! Ulla retorted: "Do you suppose that he was one for whom a defence could be made? Was he not a *Mesith* [enticer], concerning whom Scripture says, *Neither shalt thou spare, neither shalt thou conceal him.* With Yeshu however it was different, for he was connected with the government" [or royalty, i.e., influential].[22]

The Jewish Encyclopedia, citing the Talmud, says that Jesus was like Balaam, a false prophet, seducing men and leading them to idolatrous practices, and that ". . . the pseudonym 'Balaam,' [is] given to Jesus in Sanh. 106*b* and Git. 57*a*."[23] Another quotation from the same source goes like this:

Jesus is accordingly in the following curious Talmudic legend thought to sojourn in hell. A certain Onkelos B. Kalonikos son of Titus's sister, desired to embrace Judaism, and called up from hell by magic first Titus, then Balaam, and finally Jesus, who are here taken as the worst enemies of Judaism. He asked Jesus: "Who is esteemed in that world?" Jesus said: "Israel." "Shall one join them?" Jesus said to him: "Further their well-being; do nothing to their detriment; whoever touches them touches the apple of His eye." Onkelos then asked the nature of his punishment, and was told that it was the degrading fate of those who mock the wise. (Git. 56*b*–57*a*)[24]

Gittin 56*b*-57*a* in the Babylonian Talmud states:

Whoever mocks at the words of the Sages is punished with boiling hot excrement.[25]

Many evangelicals use Zechariah 2:8, concerning "the apple of His eye," in the same way that the Talmudists apply it in the above passage. They are failing to see that the Church inherits many of these Old Testament promises and that God's love is universal and impartial.

Another biblical passage, John 9:31, has been misinterpreted by a number of evangelicals who have been influenced by pharisaic teaching. The passage reads:

> Now we know that God does not hear sinners; but if anyone is a worshiper of God and does His will, He hears him.

Many evangelical teachers and preachers contend that God does not hear the prayer of sinners on the basis of this passage. The verse does not say that God Himself was declaring that He will not hear the prayer of sinners, but the Pharisees were teaching that erroneous doctrine. The reason for this is that they were accusing the Lord Jesus of being a sinner and a false Messiah according to their Talmudic teaching. God loves to hear the prayer of sinners who come to Him with repentant hearts as the publican did in saying, "God be merciful to me a sinner" (Luke 18:13). That sinner went to his home justified, but the prideful prayer of the Pharisee was unheard.

Defenders of Orthodox Judaism become very upset when anyone critically examines the Talmud. The slightest negative observation is called anti-Semitic. If that is the case, then the Lord Jesus was anti-Semitic when He told the Pharisees,

> You are of your father the devil, and the desires of your father you want to do. He does not stand in the truth, because there is no truth in him. . . . He who is of God hears God's words; therefore you do not hear, because you are not of God. (John 8:44–47)

In other passages He said to the Pharisees:

> But woe to you, scribes and Pharisees, hypocrites! For you shut up the kingdom of heaven against men; for you neither go in yourselves, nor do you allow those who are entering to go in. Woe to you, scribes and Pharisees, hypocrites! For you devour widow's houses, and for a pretense make long prayers, therefore you will receive greater condemnation. . . . Woe to you, scribes and Phari-

sees, hypocrites! For you are like whitewashed tombs which indeed appear beautiful outwardly, but inside are full of dead men's bones. . . . Serpents, brood of vipers! How can you escape the condemnation of hell? (Matt. 23:13–33)

I know that you are Abraham's descendants, but you seek to kill Me, because My word has no place in you. . . . If God were your Father, you would love Me. . . . You are of your father the devil. (John 8:37–44)

These verses are applicable also to every monotheistic religious leader who does not believe that the Lord Jesus is the only "way, the truth, and the life," and that no one could go to heaven except through Him (John 14:6). Such people will keep others from entering heaven by "making the word of God of no effect through [their] tradition that [they] have handed down" (Mark 7:13).

It was one of the saddest moments of the Lord's earthly ministry when "He came to His own, and His own did not receive Him" (John 1:11). The reason His own people did not receive Him was because He claimed to be equal with God. They accused Him of having a demon (John 7:20), and on many occasions they sought to kill Him (John 7:1, 19). Nevertheless, in spite of their outright hostility and their relentless efforts to undermine His sovereign authority, the Lord is grieved not about His personal rejection, but about their rejection of His salvation. He was not willing that anyone of them "should perish but that all should come to repentance" (2 Pet. 3:9).

We have seen from the foregoing that the Talmud is not inspired by God; neither did God promise to bless or curse those who are kind or unkind to Israel. Nonetheless, Christians must not curse anyone. We are commanded to love even the unloveable. The Lord Jesus said:

Love your enemies, bless those who curse you, do good to those who hate you, and pray for those who spitefully use you and persecute you, that you may be sons of your Father in heaven; for He makes His sun rise on the evil and on the good, and sends rain on the just and on the unjust. For if you love those who love you, what reward have you? (Matt. 5:44–46)

The Alliance in Action

Ariel Sharon masterminded the Israeli invasion of Lebanon in 1982. More than 200,000 persons were killed and wounded. Most of them were civilians, among whom were some of our relatives. Ironically, the invasion of Lebanon was hailed by Christian Zionists as a fulfillment of prophecy. Ariel Sharon was proclaimed as the person whom God had divinely called and appointed to reclaim the Promised Land from the Arabs.

My wife and I were invited in 1991 by the president of The Religious Roundtable to make a special trip to Israel along with Christian and Jewish leaders. The purpose of the visit was to exhibit love and concern for the Jews. We were also told that Ariel Sharon and other Israeli politicians would be the key speakers.

My wife and I were very excited about the trip to the land where our Lord was born and about the unique opportunity for us to meet top Israeli government officials. After we landed in Tel Aviv, we were driven by bus to the luxurious Hyatt Regency Hotel in Jerusalem. The moment we arrived at the main entrance of the hotel I noticed a large plaque with the words: WELCOME, AMERICAN RELIGIOUS LEADERS IN SOLIDARITY WITH ISRAEL.

The following day we heard many Israeli speakers emphasizing the central conviction of political Zionism. Then, Ariel Sharon presented a theological rendition in favor of Israel, and everyone gave him a standing ovation except my wife and me. However, we were given enough grace to forgive Sharon for his wicked deeds against our people, and we prayed for his salvation.

Strangely, the pastors and other Christian leaders who were afforded the opportunity to address the crowd promoted

43

a physical Israel and political Zionism instead of sharing the gospel of Christ with the Israelis. One Christian speaker said,

> This land is for Israel not the land of Ishmael, and if the Jews don't succeed in expelling the Palestinians in this generation, it will be done in the next generation.

We heard many comments of this kind and were grief-stricken to hear such harmful words from our brothers and sisters in Christ. Also, some Christian Zionists told the Jews who were present to annex the West Bank and urged them to live exclusively among the Jews, mainly because:

> God didn't have them [Palestinians] in His master plan. His concern was for the Jews, to whom He had given the Holy Land.[26]

Two

THE LAND OF CANAAN

During previous missionary travels to Europe, I was introduced to a converted Palestinian Muslim medical doctor living in Vienna, Austria. He had read my book *Understanding the Arab World* and was interested in translating it into Arabic for the benefit of his people.

Abdallah shared with me how he had lost his profession, his property, his family and had suffered unjustly at the hands of the Israeli government. His predicament was most depressing. His housing was of the lowest quality in Vienna. His income was extremely meager. "How," I asked him, "has a professional medical man been reduced to such a deplorable situation?" Abdallah then began to recount his story.

The government of Israel singled out Palestinian leaders from all walks of life and used coercive methods to uproot them from their homeland. Those who refused to leave were punished. In Abdallah's case this punishment took the form of imprisonment, torture, expropriation of his property, and violation of his young wife.

His ancestral home was dynamited and his lands were confiscated. Similar stories have been advanced by many Palestinians who have been forcefully expatriated. Shortly thereafter while imprisoned, he was beaten and both arms were broken. This effectively ended his medical practice.

The roots of the Palestinians' predicament can be traced to the misinterpretation of Noah's curse on Canaan and also to the promises God made to Abraham concerning the land of Canaan.

Many Christian publications have attempted to define the chronic conflict existing between the Palestinians and the Israelis. Some have been courageous enough to offer reasonable and equitable solutions, but the majority of them have been unable to present a balanced view of the eschatological and historical background of both the land and the contestants. Instead, in support of Israel they have laid claim on the biblical covenant of Genesis 17:8, where God had promised Abraham and his descendants "all the land of Canaan as an everlasting possession."

Major Christian leaders and others have tenaciously declared that the Scriptures support the concept of a Jewish homeland and the expulsion of the Palestinians from their native country—called the "Holy Land". This teaching rests mainly on the fact that there is no biblical proof of the Palestinians' lineage from Abraham. That kind of argument has encouraged the continued support of the Jewish occupation of the land by coercion and the ongoing expansionism instigated by each succeeding Israeli government. That distorted interpretation of biblical prophecy has caused untold human suffering and has contributed to the turmoil in the Middle East. A more careful study of the Bible will reveal that God's plans include both Arabs and Jews, and that study must begin with Noah's curse on Canaan in Genesis 9:20–21 to determine whether the curse falls on the land, the inhabitants of the land, or both.

The Prophecy of Noah

The story of the land of Canaan goes back to earliest times in biblical history. The first mention of Canaan in the Bible occurs in Genesis 9:18: "And the sons of Noah who went out of the ark were Shem, Ham, and Japheth. And Ham was the father of Canaan." Canaan was the son of Ham and the grandson of Noah. This is evidently an important fact due to the numerous references in Scripture to Canaan, the land of

Canaan, and Canaanites. The ensuing account in Genesis concerns the drunkenness of Noah, the viewing of Noah by Ham, and Noah's curse on Canaan. Noah's curse is in the form of a prophecy because Canaan probably had not been born when the prophecy was made. Does it refer to the grandson of Noah, the land itself, or the descendants of Canaan who occupied the land? The entire curse passage is as follows:

> And Noah began to be a farmer, and he planted a vineyard. Then he drank of the wine and was drunk, and became uncovered in his tent. And Ham, the father of Canaan, saw the nakedness of his father, and told his two brothers outside. But Shem and Japheth took a garment, laid it on both their shoulders, and went backward and covered the nakedness of their father. Their faces were turned away, and they did not see their father's nakedness. So Noah awoke from his wine, and knew what his younger son had done to him. Then he said: "Cursed be Canaan; A servant of servants He shall be to his brethren." And he said: "Blessed be the Lord, The God of Shem, And may Canaan be his servant, May God enlarge Japheth, And may he dwell in the tents of Shem; And may Canaan be his servant." (Gen. 9:20–27)

The Curse on Canaan

Noah's curse on Canaan has puzzled Bible students for centuries, mainly because it is hard to understand why Canaan was blamed for his father's sin. When Scripture teaches that sin is passed down from generation, to generation it is referring to one of two things: either the Adamic sin nature, or the consequences of the fathers' sins on their children, as the second commandment indicates:

> For I, the Lord your God, am a jealous God, visiting the iniquity of the fathers upon the children to the third and fourth generations of those who hate Me, but showing mercy to thousands, to those who love Me and keep My commandments. (Exod. 20:5–6)

47

In this passage, the Lord provides a route of escape to all those who love Him and keep His commandments. (The Lord Jesus paraphrased this passage in John 14:15 as instructions to His disciples.) The Prophet Jeremiah also taught individual responsibility before the judgment of God, not simply a judgment due to inheritance:

> In those days they shall say no more: "The fathers have eaten sour grapes, And the children's teeth are set on edge." But every one shall die for his own iniquity; every man who eats the sour grapes, his teeth shall be set on edge. (Jer. 31:29–30)

Canaan probably was not born at the time the curse was pronounced. Only eight persons were saved out of the Flood: Noah, Shem, Ham, Japheth, and their wives. The three sons of Noah most likely did not have any children at the time Noah's curse on Canaan occurred. If they did, the children would have been babies, for Noah planted his vineyard right after the Flood. The time for the grape vines to mature, the grapes to be picked, and the wine to ferment would add up to only a few years.

A divine purpose guided Noah's lips in the curse, for this pronouncement prepared the way for Abraham and the twelve tribes of Israel concerning the land of Canaan. Attempting to understand the divine purpose behind Noah's curse has led to different reasons for Canaan, and not Ham, being cursed. Some have suggested that the curse is applicable to the Blacks, due to their historical evidence of servitude and present ethnic predicament. Others maintain that Noah's curse on Canaan is a prophetic statement regarding Ham's moral guilt that would manifest itself in Canaan and his posterity. A third view, which I propose, concerns the land of Canaan, and is not necessarily related to Canaan personally or to his descendants.

Genesis 9:20–27 may be divided in numerous ways, but one good outline makes verses 20–21 the first major division of the passage. These verses show how a great man of God became the main cause of the problem. Noah had the ideal opportunity to establish a healthy society after the Flood, but instead he "was found drunk in his tent."[1] Verses 22–23 mark the second division and record the reaction of Noah's three sons to his unfortunate sin of drunkenness. The third division, verses 24–27, details the famous prophetic announcement of cursing and blessing by Noah.

One critical point is whether the Hebrew text supports the idea of the curse falling on Canaan or whether it falls on Ham. The editors of *Biblia Hebraica* have a footnote stating that one Greek manuscript has Ham. The Arabic version also supports the reading of Ham in the text of Genesis 9:25, reading for Canaan *pater Canaan*, (father of Canaan) rather than simply Canaan.[2] In Calvin's commentary on Genesis, his editor wrote:

> And on this authority of the Arabic version (see Walton's Polygott), many learned men would thus fill up the line . . . "Cursed be Ham, the father of Canaan." They would also, on the same authority, alter the fourth and sixth lines by inserting the word "father," thus . . . "And let the father of Canaan be their servant."[3]

Although the Arabic reading is more consistent than the Greek, neither were considered reliable by Rahlf's critical Septuagint. Also against this rendering is the plain reading of the Hebrew text of the Massoretes, which states in Genesis 9:25 "cursed be Canaan."[4] In this passage the word *cursed* is a verbal form from the passive participle of the root *to curse*. The participle in the active voice suggests the subject acting. The passive voice suggests action happening to the subject. The continuous action is taking place on Canaan the subject of the verbal noun clause. The participle stresses a durative quality pointing primarily to the land, because with the death of Canaan the durative quality would cease. However, the application of the curse continues with respect to the land.

The remainder of 9:25 describes what the curse involves: "a servant of servants he shall be to his brethren." "Servant of servants" expresses the superlative in Hebrew,[5] a common expression in Hebrew found in such phrases as vanity of vanities, song of songs, Lord of lords, King of kings, and Holy of Holies.

The Blessing on Shem

In verse 26, Noah continues his prophecy by pronouncing a blessing upon Shem. In this passage we see a balance of divine blessing and cursing. The blessing is also in the form of a passive participle and its durative action has the same meaning as it did in the cursing of Canaan. Thus, the verbal noun brings into view the descendants of Shem. In fact Shem was not blessed in verse 26, but the coming Messiah was blessed. The blessing here may be interpreted, "Blessed be Jehovah, the God of Shem."[6]

In verse 27, the blessing is extended to the descendants of Japheth, meaning that they are going to be partakers of the spiritual blessings of Shem. Speaking about the Messianic prophecy in Genesis, Schaeffer asserted:

> The first Messianic prophecy is Genesis 3:15, that the seed of the woman shall bruise the serpent's head. . . . Later it becomes clear that this one who will fulfill Genesis 3:15 will come through the line of Seth and not through the line of Cain.

And in the present passage, Genesis 9:26–27, are further details:

> And he said: "Blessed be Jehovah, the God of Shem; and let Canaan be his servant. God enlarge Japheth, And let him dwell in the tents of Shem" (ASV). In other words, the promise that was first given to all men is now narrowed to the Semitic peoples. . . . Genesis makes plain that though the promise will be fulfilled through the Semitic people, it is actually open to the whole human race.[7]

The Palestinian version of the Talmud sees the prophecy of blessing being fulfilled in the revelation of the Messiah. Thus, Shem was blessed with the knowledge of a saving faith in Jehovah, and Japheth was given a promise to share in spiritual advantages.

The Meaning of the Prophecy

Whatever else is intimated in Noah's cursing and blessing, damnation and salvation are there. In other words, since the whole earth was populated from the three sons of Noah (Gen. 9:19), and since the Old Testament is replete with typology, God has chosen to use Noah's prophetic utterances in order to fulfill His good purposes for the human race in relation to eternal salvation as opposed to eternal damnation.

To say it differently, all those who believe in the Lord God of Shem will receive eternal salvation, and those who reject the free gift of salvation will be damned. Ham was included among the eight persons that were saved out of the Flood; therefore individuals from the whole human race typified by these three sons are recipients of God's saving grace. Canaan is a type of unregenerate man, while Shem and Japheth are types of God's spiritual blessing.

Noah's three sons along with his grandson Canaan were used by God to show the principle behind God's curse or blessing. Some will be declared righteous by believing and trusting God the Redeemer for salvation; others will be declared unrighteous through rejection of the Seed of the woman (Christ) who would bruise the head of the serpent (Gen. 3:15). This principle is clearly seen in the Acts of the Apostles, where God demonstrated His indiscriminate love for the human race by saving one descendant from each of the three sons of Noah. The Ethiopian eunuch was a descendant of Ham (Acts 8:26–39); Saul of Tarsus was a descendant of Shem (Acts 9:1–19); and Cornelius was a descendant of Japheth (Acts 10). Whereas the prophecy of Genesis 3:15 is applicable to the whole human race, the blessing on Shem concerns the physical lineage of the Messiah.

Perhaps God extended the blessing to the descendants of Japheth because He knew that the Jews would reject the Messiah, and the responsibility of spreading the gospel of Christ would be given to the Gentiles (John 1:11–13; cf. Matt. 21:43). In that sense, Japheth was a prototype of the Gentile world.

> The blessing of Shem was tied in a peculiar way to a covenant relationship with God, as indicated by the use of the extended term "Lord God," which is a covenant title. However, by inspiration, Noah was able to foretell that this covenant relationship would in some way be interrupted . . . so that Japheth would one day assume the responsibility which had been divinely appointed to Shem.[8]

Many Bible scholars agree that Noah's curse on Canaan had far-reaching prophetic implications. Unger stated:

> Curses delivered against individuals by holy men (Gen. 9:25, 49:7; Deut. 27:15; Josh. 6:26) are not the expressions of revenge, passion, or impatience; they are predictions, and, therefore, not such as God condemns.[9]

Lloyd agrees with Unger in that, "Noah spoke by the Spirit of prophecy."[10] Keil and Delitzsh also agree that "words of blessing and curse . . . were prophetic."[11] It would seem possible that Noah's cursing and blessing were prophetic in nature and extended to the posterity of Canaan, Shem, and Japheth in terms of salvation and damnation.

The curse on Canaan is on all those who do not believe in the Lord God of Shem for salvation. The verbal nouns of cursing and blessing undergird this view by suggesting a continuation from generation to generation, affecting the descendants of Noah's three sons. This of course means that descendants from all the sons of Noah will be among the saved and the damned.

52

A Brief History of the Canaanites
From the dawn of recorded history (around 3000 B.C.), the Canaanites occupied Lebanon, Western Syria, and Palestine.

They probably came in the same wave of migration that brought the Amorites from the Arabian desert and spilled them over the Fertile Crescent. The origin of the Canaanites is recorded in Genesis 10:6: "The sons of Ham were Cush, Mizraim, Put, and Canaan." All the direct descendants of Canaan are listed in Genesis 10:15–18.

The Canaanites are often mentioned in the Scriptures as one of the people living side by side with the Hittites and the Amorites and the Perizzites and the Hivites and the Jebusites (Exod. 3:8). Yet, all these peoples were at times identified as Canaanites and shared many common traditions, as seen in their racial blending. "The Canaanites were called Phoenicians by the Greeks, and later the term Phoenician became synonymous with Canaanites."[12] The most popular cities of the Phoenician civilization were Byblos, Sidon, and Tyre, all of which had close commercial and social ties with Egypt and Israel. The Phoenician civilization produced an alphabet of twenty-two consonants from which the principal ancient and modern alphabets are derived. The Phoenicians helped King Solomon build his ships and train his navy in the knowledge of the sea (1 Kings 9:27, 10:22) and they were the first shipbuilders to cross the Mediterranean Sea and the Atlantic (at least to England) in search of iron ore, copper, tin, and gold. Ezekiel 27:12 seems to link Tarshish with the Canaanites (Phoenicians).

Although this study concerns the prophetic implications of Noah's curse on Canaan, the three sons of Noah play a historical and prophetic role in the fulfillment of the prophecy. *Tarshish* is a Phoenician term meaning "sea merchants or traders." Ancient Tartassos (modern Cadiz) is derived from the word Tarshish. Tartassos, a city in southern Spain, had been used by the Phoenicians as a commercial seaport for cargo ships. Tarshish was the second son of Javan and a grandson of Japheth (Gen. 10:4). Many Bible scholars and reliable historians believe that Spain was founded by Tarshish. Spain became identified with sea merchants and traders, and Tarshish became a mecca for the Phoenicians.

History books record that while the Phoenicians were sailing to England in search of tin, they discovered many lands. They founded and colonized Gades (modern Gibraltar), a town on the southern rocky tip of Spain. They also founded and colonized Carthage (modern Tunisia), Sardinia (near Italy), Tartassos (modern Cadiz in Spain), and others. Both Amerigo Vespucci and Christopher Columbus used maritime skills and geographic knowledge developed by the genius of the Phoenicians. Spain was credited with the discovery of the Americas, but the Phoenicians, or Canaanites, contributed the basic crafts required for such great accomplishments, as their technological genius shows:

> Canaan was advanced in material culture. Cities were well laid out, and houses showed good design and construction. Floors of buildings were often paved or plastered. Workers were skilled in the use of copper, lead, and gold. Pottery was among the finest anywhere in the world. . . . In technical knowledge, Canaanites were much in advance of Israelites who had spent the past forty years in nomadic conditions of the desert. . . . History shows that less developed cultures are normally absorbed by those more advanced.[13]

God gave distinct blessings to the three sons of Noah. Salvation by faith in Christ came through Shem; technology came through Ham; philosophy and logic came through Japheth, particularly with respect to his descendants through Javan who became the father of the Greeks (Gen. 10:2), such as Plato, Socrates, and Aristotle. The contributions of the descendants of Shem, Ham, and Japheth bear witness to that fact. In this sense, Noah's prophecy that Canaan would be a servant of servants was literally fulfilled. The Canaanites made tremendous technological contributions to world civilization. The Puritans might have spoken of these contributions as common grace, a blessing from God that benefits both lost and saved alike. So these Canaanite servants did indeed serve the world by producing technical advances for the benefit of mankind.

54

Divine Right to the Promised Land

The Land of Canaan has been erroneously called the "Holy Land." There is nothing holy about the land itself. Our Lord lamented over her saying, "O Jerusalem, Jerusalem, the one who kills the prophets and stones those who are sent to her" (Matt. 23:37). In fact, it should now be called "the bloody land", because much blood has been shed on it and many unholy things have been practiced there. Bloody wars and inhumane treatment continue to occur in that land.

Unholy wars bathed the Promised Land with human blood. Pregnant women and children were massacred. Old folks were butchered, and families were burned alive. It is amazing that all this was done in the name of God and blessed by the highest religious leaders. In the future, according to the New Testament, the land and its people will go through a great tribulation, "such as has not been since the beginning of the world" (Matt. 24:21; cf. Dan. 12:1–3). When our Lord will send Moses and Elijah back to Jerusalem to preach the gospel, they will be killed. "And their dead bodies will lie in the street of the great city which spiritually is called Sodom and Egypt, where also our Lord was crucified" (Rev. 11:8). From the foregoing, we learn that the Promised Land is not holy, and the earthly Jerusalem is called Sodom.

Only our God is holy, not the land. The Promised Land has been appointed unto destruction along with the whole earth since the time of Adam. God said to Adam,

> Because you have heeded the voice of your wife, and have eaten from the tree of which I commanded you saying, "You shall not eat of it": cursed is the ground for your sake. (Gen. 3:17)

The whole earth is under the curse of God until its final destruction when its "elements will melt with fervent heat" (2 Pet. 3:10) unable to withstand God's judgment (cf. Rev. 20:11). The Promised Land shall become holy when the Holy City is revealed, "coming down out of heaven from God" (Rev. 21:2).

It is interesting to note how man was able to devise various and sanctimonious ways to justify his conquests by appealing to the holy Scripture or other religious books to put God on his side. For example, the Crusaders slaughtered thousands of Arabs and Jews in the Middle East in the name of Christ. Their counterparts fought many religious wars during the Reformation in Europe and spread these to the Americas, Australia, and Africa. Indeed religion supported the slaughter of the American Indians and the resurgence of slavery in the New World. Islam, in the name of Allah, rapidly grew by the sword.

In the name of God, a white ruling party in South Africa instituted the apartheid regime. In the name of God, international conflicts and war become more inspiring to most Christians and others than does a biblical mandate to decency, compassion, and love of neighbor. In the name of God, the land promised to Abraham in Genesis 12:1 becomes misinterpreted as a biblical mandate for total commitment to Israel's aggression.

The current Middle East turmoil cannot be grasped without recognizing that a major disturbing element has been ignorance of precisely what the Bible has promised and to whom the land was divinely ordained. With the continued expansion of Israel, the question must be raised as to whether the Jews have an exclusive divine right to the Promised Land, or was this right the result of political pressure and military conquest.

The country that the Israelites wrested from its inhabitants and seized for their own habitat is in many ways a remarkable region. Its biblical importance overshadows its small territorial extent. Palestine, which is now called Israel, is about the size of the state of New Jersey. Its length from north to south is about 180 miles, and its breadth from east to west, about 45 miles, thus giving the tiny country an area of only 8,000 square miles. Jordan bounds it on the east, Lebanon on the north, the Sinai Desert on the south, and the Mediterranean Sea on the west.

I believe God gave the land of Canaan to the Jews for three distinct prophetic purposes:

1. To pave the way for the Incarnation of His son, Jesus Christ. God said that out of Bethlehem "shall come forth to Me the One to be ruler in Israel, Whose goings forth have been from of old, from everlasting" (Mic. 5:2). His first coming to Palestine forms the golden thread that extends through and binds together all the books of the Old Testament into one principal theme, which was fulfilled at the cross of Calvary. Man's redemption through the atoning death of Christ is the most important doctrine of the entire Bible.

2. God has predetermined to judge all Jews and Gentiles who have failed to believe in the sin-bearing Messiah at the time of His glorious return, by allowing them to experience the horror of "Jacob's trouble" (Jer. 30:7), "such as never was since there was a nation, even to that time" (Dan. 12:1). The Lord Jesus said that everyone who willfully rejects His substitutionary death and remains alive during such a time will go through the great tribulation, "such as has not been since the beginning of the world until this time, no, nor ever shall be" (Matt. 24:21). Thus, God gave the land of Palestine to the Jews in order that He "will gather all the nations to battle against Jerusalem" (Zech. 14:2).

3. The Lord Jesus will return to Jerusalem, the same land so set aside for judgment, to reign "for a thousand years" over the whole earth (Rev. 20:4). Only then, "Jerusalem shall be safely inhabited" (Zech. 14:11)! This blessed historical event will take place about one thousand years prior to the great White Throne Judgment of the unsaved. The reader will do well to listen to the words of John the Beloved:

Then I saw a great white throne and Him who sat on it, from whose face the earth and the heaven fled away. And there was found no place for them. And I saw the dead, small and great, standing before God, and books were opened. And another book was opened, which is the book of life. And the dead were judged according to their works, by the things which were written in the books. The sea gave up the dead who were in it, and death and Hades delivered up the dead who were in them. And they were judged, each one according to his works. Then death and Hades were cast into the lake of fire. This is the second death. And anyone not found written in the book of life was cast into the lake of fire. (Rev. 20:11–15)

Just because God initially gave the land of Canaan to the Jews for prophetic reasons, this does not necessarily give them the continuing, exclusive, divine right to use military coercive measures against the Palestinians in order to up-root them from their habitat.

The Book of Genesis records that Abraham became the father of many nations, including the eighteen Arabian nations, through Hagar and Keturah (Gen. 17:20, 25:1–2). The Palestinians seem to be included in the promise of God to Abraham when He said He was going to give the land to his descendants "as an everlasting possession" (Gen. 17:8). The Palestinians are an offshoot of the Philistines, who descended from Mizraim, the second son of Ham (Gen. 10:6, 13–14). Mizraim founded Egypt, and the Palestinians may have had their roots in a splinter group from an Egyptian branch through intermarriage.

The promise was made before the births of Ishmael and Isaac. The only time the land was under an exclusive Jewish control was during the period of King Solomon's rule (1 Kings 4:21). In other words, the Palestinians and other Arabs have always lived side by side with the Jews in the Promised Land!

Even though God is sovereignly regathering the Jews to the Promised Land in order to prepare the world for the great tribulation, Israel has forfeited the promises of God by disobeying His commandments. Conversely, God promised a New Covenant to be written not on tables of stone, but to be written in the hearts of His people, "the Israel of God" (Gal. 6:16). In place of military victory over human enemies, the Lord Jesus gives victory over sin and death. In place of the land of Canaan, He gives us His kingdom as an inheritance. In place of milk and honey, He gives us the fruit of the Holy Spirit to love our enemies, to bless those who curse us, to do good to those who hate us, and to pray for those who spitefully use us and persecute us (Matt. 5:44)!

Abolishment of All Curses

Noah's curse on Canaan is not directly related to any particular segment of the human race, and any such view is man's way of justifying his own pride and prejudice. The deep-rooted racial problems between Arabs and Jews and between other groups might be alleviated if the Christian world would take a closer look at New Testament truths.

While the earth remains under the curse of God (Gen. 3:17), the death of Christ on the cross has abolished the curse on Canaan and his descendants. Anyone who comes to God through Christ the Savior, irrespective of nationality, becomes a child of God. Paul in Galatians 3:26–29 concurs with this truth: "For you are all sons of God through faith in Christ Jesus. . . . And if you are Christ's, then you are Abraham's seed, and heirs according to the promise" (cf. Gen. 12:3; Rom. 4:11). The only persons who are still under the curse of God are those who have not yet been regenerated, as John said:

> He who believes in the Son has everlasting life; and he who does not believe the Son shall not see life, but the wrath of God abides on him (John 3:36; cf. 8:39–47).

Noah's curse on Canaan is never mentioned in the New Testament because the curse was typological and prophetic, not racial. It is related to salvation and damnation.

The curse is twofold: first, the curse falls on the land of Canaan, not people; and second, Noah's curse and blessing are an Old Testament type of salvation and damnation.

Three

UNHOLY WARS

Man has been conditioned by his ethnic heritage and by his own cultural upbringing to interpret and to internalize his religious beliefs logically in a manner that seems to put God on his side. Although I have tried to be objective in my presentation of this topic, the reader may notice a somewhat subjective view of the Arabs. The reason for this is that man tends to sympathize with his own cultural heritage. These cultural views have the power to mold his attitudes, shape his character and beliefs, and guide his thoughts and actions. Even Flavius Josephus, the famous Jewish historian, "was doubtless writing to honor his fellow countrymen and to defend Judaism."[1] Nevertheless, I am constrained by bonds of love not to compromise with the claims of Christ, because my faith in Him is undergirded by an unswerving commitment to His infallible Word.

Judaism, Christianity, and Islam believe that God has intervened directly in their behalf in many events to help them win their holy wars. God does indeed intervene in human affairs in order to fulfill His sovereign purpose. God exercises His will historically and prophetically. History is the stage on which God plays out His prophetic plan for the human race. Thus, the whole world, including the countries embracing one or more of the three monotheistic religions, participates involuntarily in the drama of wars and rumors of wars (Matt. 24:6). When we look at the world around us, we see that history is repeating itself in a long tale of man's inhumanity to man. Spain had its Inquisition, Britain its Atlantic slave trade, Germany its gas chambers, Russia its Siberian labor camps, the United States its Indian reservations, Iraq its chemical and biological weapons; and the world is still swept by fear, lust, greed, and racial tension.

Man has been unable to live peaceably with his fellow-man because of his total depravity and his manifest failure to follow the teachings of Christ. For instance, the Lord Jesus taught in the Sermon on the Mount, "But I say to you, love your enemies, bless those who curse you, do good to those who hate you, and pray for those who spitefully use you and persecute you" (Matt. 5:44); and again He taught, "But I tell you not to resist an evil person. But whoever slaps you on your right cheek, turn the other to him also" (Matt. 5:39).

There have been individuals, such as St. Francis of Assisi, who have been able to live out Christ's teachings, but most would rather kill the enemy than turn the other cheek.

Religious leaders must consider their words when dealing with their all-too-human flocks. It is much easier to vilify the enemy in the name of God than to practice the teachings of Jesus. The Crusades are but one example of mankind's choice not to exercise self-control, but to give in to the desires of the flesh.

The Seed of Holy Wars

The seed of holy wars between the three monotheistic religions is found in the original promise of God to Abraham when He appeared to him and said, "To your descendants I will give this land" (Gen. 12:7). Abraham's descendants have been fighting holy wars for that land ever since.

The Jews believed that the land was exclusively theirs, and their first ruthless war of extermination was with the Canaanites who had lived there for many centuries. The Jews wanted to annihilate the Canaanites, who had become the enemies of God because of their fertility cults and idolatrous worship. In a Jewish holy war, there was no room for negotiation of peaceful coexistence or peace treaties. Truly, these early Canaanite wars were sanctioned by the commandment of God. As the Israelites entered the Promised Land, Joshua was instructed to annihilate the inhabitants. This was done to secure the land and to punish the wickedness of the Canaanites. Men, women, children, and animals were annihilated on many occasions. For example, after the Jews massacred all that were living in Ai, then Joshua wiped out "the Anakim . . . from Hebron, from Debir, from Anab, from all the mountains of Judah, and from all the mountains of Israel: [he] utterly destroyed them with their cities. . . . None of the Anakim were left in the land" (Josh. 11:21–22; cf. 8:24–25, 28).

However since the time of Joshua until now, the Jews have established a pattern of ruthless military wars for the world to emulate. The problem with this is that there is no mandate from God for Jews, nor Gentiles, to establish a pattern of genocidal killing. That mandate ended with the establishment of Old Testament Israel in the land. The holy war that occurred in the Joshua passages was sanctioned for one specific people against another specific people. It was limited in time and place. Since that time holy war is contrary to God's will.

Because of their disobedience to God's commandments concerning idolatry and false worship, the Jews had to experience the horror of exile and persecution. They even had to eat their own children in time of famine as it was predicted by Ezekiel, "Therefore the fathers shall eat the sons in the midst of thee, and the sons shall eat their fathers. . . ." (Ezek. 5:10; and also by Moses in Lev. 26:27–29; and in Deut. 28:53–57). This prophecy was fulfilled when "Ben-Hadad king of Syria . . . besieged Samaria" (1 Kings 20:1). After the great famine came upon the Jews, one woman said to another woman, "Give your son, that we may eat him today, and we will eat my son tomorrow. So we boiled my son, and ate him" (2 Kings 6:28–29). When Israel was restored from Babylonian captivity in around 538 B.C., the wars fought were self-defensive, rather than the holy wars of earlier days.

There has been great mass-media coverage of Israel's modern wars that began in 1948 with the founding of the State of Israel. During the Suez Conflict of 1956, Israel attacked Egypt and took the whole of Sinai. As a result of American pressure, Israel withdrew. In order to short-circuit an impending Egyptian attack, Israel struck in June, 1967, occupying the whole of Sinai, the West Bank, the old city of Jerusalem, and the Golan Heights.

The Egyptians struck first in the Yom Kippur War of October, 1973. They pushed some distance into the Sinai. The Israeli counterattack encircled a large portion of the Egyptian army. This partial success made possible President Sadat's historic visit to Jerusalem in 1977. This visit eventually resulted in the Camp David Treaty of 1979. In 1978 the first invasion of Lebanon began in an attempt to defeat Palestinian forces operating out of southern Lebanon. The annexation of the Golan Heights followed in 1981, and a second invasion of Lebanon in 1982. These protracted attacks have been inherited from Old Testament practice and culture.

The holy war mentality also made its way into Christendom. Today, most of the civilized world would condemn the Christian crusaders for their holy wars of extermination against the Muslims. Like Judaism and Islam, Christianity has had an inherent appetite for violence, despite the teaching of the Lord and Savior Jesus Christ, who commanded His followers to love their enemies and to do good to those who hate them, not to exterminate them (Matt. 5:44).

The term *crusade* is derived from the French *croix*, meaning "cross". The Crusaders sewed crosses on their clothes and called themselves pilgrims. When Pope Urban II called for a holy war against Islam during the Council of Clermont on November 25, 1095, more than 100,000 men along with their wives and families responded and marched to Palestine. This was the First Crusade. The Pope urged the people of Europe to liberate the holy city of Jerusalem from the infidels and to "exterminate this vile race from our lands."[2]

Judaism, Christianity, and Islam all believe that they are historically and theologically related to Abraham and to the worship of the same God, and yet for centuries they have been slaughtering each other in the name of God, thinking that they are offering "God service" (John 16:2). All three religions are encouraged to carry out deeds of benevolence, but all three have developed a pattern of holy wars that have become a tradition of monotheism. The sixth commandment given to Moses on Mount Sinai was, "You shall not murder" (Exod. 20:13). In fact, most of the Ten Commandments are given for the benefit of the human race, but so far no nation has been able to live peaceably by obeying the commandments of God.

Western Christians have labeled Islam as "the religion of the sword," and they still believe that it is the most violent of the three monotheistic religions. This is one of the many misconceptions the *western* world has inherited from the period of the Crusades. It is true that Islam's holy wars have played a key part in the establishment and spread of its religion, but Christendom has caused more bloodshed than Islam. For instance, "There has never been an Islamic Inquisition or a Holocaust equivalent to that of Hitler's regime."[3] Christian militancy and justifiable militarism were an accepted concept during the medieval period. "Eleventh-century Christians not only accepted the idea of Christian violence: they acted upon it."[4] There is a close affinity between Christian militancy and militarism—both contend that the use of force is justifiable against the enemies of God. This concept was inherited from St. Augustine's doctrines. Augustine interpreted Jesus' parable of the banquet, "Go out into the highways and hedges, and compel them to come in" (Luke 14:23) as a justification for the use of physical force. The same text "was quoted often by ecclesiastics in the High Middle Ages— by inquisitors among others."[5] The belief that the use of force is justifiable in a holy cause is still with us today.

The warlike spirit and greed of the Crusades has been portrayed during the Gulf War of 1991 between Iraq and the

United States and its allies. More than 100,000 innocent civilians in Iraq were annihilated, after suffering the heaviest bombardment in history under the guise of a holy cause. Western powers engaged in a costly war to eject Saddam Hussein from Kuwait, but they did not raise a finger to challenge the Israeli occupation of Arab land in the West Bank and Gaza Strip. It is obvious that Western powers are interested only in protecting Israel and the oil-rich Arabs. Likewise, the recent accord, which took place on the White House lawn on September 13, 1993 between Israel and the Palestine Liberation Organization, occurred basically for the same reason: the more pacific the relations in the Middle East the more secure are the oil supplies to the West. Understanding the reasons for the holy wars of monotheism requires historical and prophetical perspective. What is the logic behind such violent atrocities against millions of innocent people? Of particular interest is the conflict over the promised land between the Jews, the Christians, and the Muslims—three great civilizations founded on religions that promoted good deeds toward their fellow men. How did they become so blinded by hatred and prejudice? Why did their religious beliefs cause them to kill one another mercilessly?

Shapers of Medieval Opinion

The teaching of the four great doctors of the early Western Church—St. Ambrose, St. Jerome, St. Augustine, and Pope Gregory the Great—molded the outlook of the medieval Christians. Ambrose, Jerome, and Augustine were born in the mid-fourth century, and Gregory was born in the mid-sixth century. The authority of these men was considered as second only to that of the Bible. Biblical scholars have always been able to influence and mold the thinking and actions of men, and the legitimate teaching of leaders has often been ruined through the excess of followers.

Ambrose

Ambrose established the independence of the church in relation to the secular state. The Crusades would have been practically impossible without a church and a Pope who could act independently of the emperor. The contest in question concern an imperial request from the Roman Empress Justina that one church in Milan, where Ambrose was bishop, should be ceded to the Arian party (those who denied the full divinity of Jesus). Ambrose stoutly refused and said in a letter to his sister:

> The counts and Tribunes came and urged me to cause the basilica to be quickly surrendered, saying that the Emperor was exercising his rights since everything was under his power. I answered that if he asked of me what was mine, that is, my land, my money, or whatever of this kind was my own, I would not refuse it, although all that I have belonged to the poor, but that those things which are God's are not subject to the imperial power. If my patrimony is required, enter upon it; if my body, I will go at once. Do you wish to cast me into chains, or to give me to death? It will be a pleasure to me. . . .[6]

Jerome

Jerome gave to the *western* world a good translation of the Bible in Latin known as the Vulgate. He also lived a life of asceticism, finally leaving Rome for Bethlehem in A.D. 386, where he remained until his death in A.D. 420. Like the desert fathers of Egypt before him, Jerome left a legacy and tradition of withdrawal from the world and living in harsh conditions in order to better seek Christ. Jerome was harsh with himself, complaining of his inability to overcome the desire to read Cicero, until he had a dream in which Christ ordered Jerome to be scourged. After this, he gave up his worldly library and no more denied Christ. Here the doctrine of purification of the flesh through voluntary suffering appears. This way of life appealed to the crusaders as a way of obtaining grace through voluntary suffering or death.

67

Augustine

The theology and philosophy of St. Augustine amplified Ambrose's stance on the relation between church and state, and virtually created the medieval view of political theory. Augustine traced the fall of man to the decadence and corruption of governments. However, even though states are infected with sin, there is a proper function that they must perform.

> We meet in St Augustine's political theory the first full explanation of society in man's fallen state. Although men are naturally social beings, had there been no fall, there would have been no need for the state, or government, as an authority imposed from above. Neither private property nor the division into masters and servants would have come about had men lived in their original state of righteousness. Peace and happiness, the desire of mankind, would have been preserved through man's own wholeness of nature. Original sin changed all this. It made necessary rulers and ruled to safeguard private property, to prevent war and disorder. Thus overlordship was a divine judgment, at once a chastisement and a remedy for sin. The state had a divine origin and rulers a divine authority. The Church was God's means of dispensing goodness; even bad rulers were the measure of society's sinfulness in calling them down upon itself.[7]

In Augustine's writings is the beginning of the tortuous medieval controversy between the sphere of authority appropriate to the church and that appropriate to the state. Also implied is the possibility of the church superseding a bad ruler in order to bring in a greater good. Here Augustine applies his doctrine of "compelling them to come in." Thus Augustine's justification of force became very influential in the medieval church.[8]

68

Gregory the Great

By the end of the sixth century, Gregory the Great (A.D. 540-604) emerged as a warrior-pope. In addition to much valuable spiritual work, Gregory personally conducted the defense of Italy against the invading Lombards.[9] Although this was a war of self-defense, we see the highest Christian leader taking up arms in a worthy cause. The precedent of warring for Christ had been established.

The Principles

The principles of withdrawal and asceticism, independence of church action, ministering good even at the point of compulsion, and warring for good causes—perhaps individually good principles—when taken together formed a stream that led to the proclamation of the First Crusade by Pope Urban II on November 25, 1095. The Pope said that the Muslims were "an accursed race, a race utterly alienated from God."[10] It was a holy act and a Christian duty to kill these godless monsters and to "exterminate this vile race from our lands."[11] The Christian crusaders were conditioned to believe that the way to paradise was through martyrdom.[12] Of course, other dynamics in the eleventh century contributed to the First Crusade.

Asceticism entered larger society in the tenth and eleventh centuries through the reforming spirit of the Benedictine monks, who encouraged pilgrimages to holy places as a practical way of lay asceticism. The passion for relics, shrines, and Jerusalem began to grow through this practical teaching for the encouragement of devotion.[13] The warrior-pope is once again reflected by Pope Urban II, and at the same time the Ambrosian idea of independence of church actions becomes a necessary part of church leadership. Indeed the church must occasionally make hard decisions that may not be approved by the secular powers. With this philosophical framework, it is easy to see why the church embraced Augustine's teaching of compulsion. Compulsion is a necessary action by state, family, or church for the greater good of the community or the good of the individual.

Principles from great teachers have a way of becoming enlarged and expounded by disciples to an extreme point that may not have been originally intended. This may have happened with the proclamation of the Crusades. However, doctrine and corresponding actions do not occur in a vacuum, but are built on previously received teaching.

The Crusades

Pope Urban II called for a holy war against the Muslims who had already conquered part of Europe and controlled the holy places in Palestine.[14] The call came at a time when Europe needed an impetus for unity. The West was also trying to forge a new image of itself, an image of vigor and action, an image of the revival of the glories of Rome, and an image to counter that of the Byzantines, who were regarded as weak and effeminate. The necessity of overcoming European feudalism required the creation of an amazing enemy, and the Muslims provided the perfect target, although most Europeans knew nothing about them. The ballads of the Franks portrayed the Muslims as idolaters who should be slaughtered with Old Testament zeal, even though handmade idols were anathema to Muslims. So the image of the Old Testament slaughter of the enemies of God was revived as part of Christian duty.

A great army was assembled in Europe to free Jerusalem from Muslim rule. The Franks decided to attack Constantinople and then to march east to Syria, so that they could cross into Palestine. When they reached Constantinople, they crossed the Bosphorus around A.D. 1097 on their way to Antioch. When the ruler of Antioch heard of their approach, he alerted the Muslims to go outside the city and dig trenches and be ready to defend the city.

When the Franks invaded Antioch and killed many Arabs, the Turkish and Arab forces in Syria rallied together and came face to face with the Frank army in front of Antioch, but the Franks defeated the Muslims and camped there for twelve days without food. Many ate their horses. After dealing this blow to the Muslims, the Franks marched on Ma'arrat an-Nu'man and besieged it. When the Franks were faced with fierce resistance, they built a wooden tower as high as the city wall and fought from the top of it. The Franks killed more than 100,000 people and took innumerable prisoners.

After the Franks defeated the Turks and Arabs at Antioch and Ma'arrat an-Nu'man, they besieged Jerusalem and fought against its inhabitants for more than six weeks. The Muslims were put to the sword and more than seventy-thousand were slaughtered, among them a large number of Jews who had lived a devout and ascetic life of pious seclusion in the holy places. The Franks then pillaged the masjid al-Aqsa and stripped the Dome of the Rock[15] of more than seventy silver and gold candelabras. The armies of the Cross showed their barbarity by killing the men and confiscating Jewish and Muslim women for their own pleasure. This kind of barbarity has been exercised by the three monotheistic religions throughout their holy wars.

With the appearance of Saladin, the real Muslim counteroffensive began. Saladin was a man of great faith in Allah. He drew his faith from reading the Qur'an in the company of scholars and devout men, and he often took part in theological discussions. His faith compelled him to obey his beliefs unto death. He loved to hear the Qur'an recited and he prayed five times a day publicly and privately. He was humble and quick to weep, but his leadership and courage in battle was without equal.

Prophet Muhammad is reported to have said, "God loves courage, even in the killing of a serpent." Saladin was indeed one of the bravest and most gallant of men regardless of the circumstances. As he was facing a great Frankish army with its reinforcements of more than seventy ships, his strength of will and tenacity of purpose increased greatly.

One day, Saladin fought a great battle on the plain of Acre, the ranks of his army were broken, drums and flags fell to the ground, but he stood firm with a handful of men. He withdrew all his men to the hill and then led them down into battle again in the name of Allah and won the victory over his enemies.

The Qur'an has many passages encouraging holy wars. Sura (Chapter) 29:69 says, "And those who fight for Our cause, We shall guide them in Our path, and God is with those who act with nobility." Another verse encourages martyrdom in a holy cause. The Qur'an says, "Who fighteth in the way of Allah be he slain or be he victorious, on him we shall bestow a vast reward."

Saladin was more zealous to die in a holy war than to die any other way. The holy war and the suffering involved in it weighed heavily on his heart. His obsession with the holy war compelled him to leave his family and his homeland. He wanted to liberate Palestine from the "idolater Christians," and to free the earth of those who do not believe in Allah. He believed that the most noble death is death in God's path (Jihad). Sura 16:3 says; "They fought for God's cause, and endured, and your Lord is forgiving and merciful."

Saladin fell ill as he was preparing for another battle against the Franks. In spite of his painful malady, he mounted his horse and ordered his troops to march to Nazareth. When the Franks heard of his illness, they went forth to strike a blow at the Muslims. Suffering as he was, he stationed his army so as to attack from the enemy's rear. He would advance a little and then dismount to rest, putting a handkerchief over his head to shield him from the heat of the sun. He refused to rest while his troops were fighting, and his army followed him to victory.

One of his memorable battles was that of Tiberias. Saladin reviewed his army of about twelve-thousand cavalry men composed of regulars and volunteers. He put them in battle order with a central column and two wings, a vanguard, and a rear guard. He assigned to each man a post and delivered a stirring speech, then led his troops and encamped near the hills of Tiberias.

When the Franks saw the Muslim army was ready to attack them, they were demoralized from fear of being slaughtered. Their fears were realized on Thursday, July 2, 1187. Saladin attacked the Franks with all his forces and took the city by storm. The city was sacked and burned, and thousands fled for refuge. The battle raged furiously for two days with both sides fighting tenaciously. The Muslim archers sent up clouds of arrows, killing many Franks and their horses. The Franks tried to fight their way out in the hope of reaching water because they were suffering greatly from thirst. But Saladin planted himself and his army in the way. Saladin's nephew performed prodigious feats of valor and he led a section of the Muslim army through the ranks of the Franks. It was so hot that one of the volunteers had set fire to the dry grass that covered the ground, and the wind carried the heat and smoke down on the Franks. Both Franks and the Muslims had to endure the summer's heat, the blazing fire and smoke, thirst, and the fury of battle; yet they believed that they were fighting in the path of their God.

The Franks were on the verge of surrender, but they tried to defy death by making a series of charges, and each wave of attackers was slaughtered by the Muslims. No one knows how many died in that battle. It has been said that blood flowed like a river. When Saladin witnessed the downfall of the Franks, he rounded up all the prisoners that were the fiercest fighters of all the Frankish warriors and he had these men decapitated. It has been reported that a year later Tiberias was still covered with their bones.

Among the things the Muslims took from Tiberias was the "true cross." It was to this particular cross to which the crusaders bowed their heads and prostrated themselves. They maintained that it was made of the exact wood of the cross of Jesus Christ. They venerated it and prostrated themselves before it. They had housed it in a casing of gold adorned with pearls and gems and kept it ready for the festival of the Passion. The cross was a prize without equal, for it was the supreme object of their faith. They offered up their lives for it and adored it. Naturally, this caused the Muslims to view Christianity as a rather gross form of idolatry.

Saladin's objective was to purify the holy land of all impure races, and this has been the intention of many religious leaders of the three monotheistic religions. After Saladin had completed his conquest of Tiberias, he conquered Ascalon and marched to Jerusalem where the Crusaders and their counterparts mounted the walls of Jerusalem and resolved to defend the city unto death.

The Muslims besieged Jerusalem for five days, and Saladin rode round the city to decide on the best way for the attack. The city was strongly defended by the Franks, mainly because the Church of the Resurrection was located there, and the Franks performed their penance and received their salvation and blessings there. Jerusalem was the place of the crucifixion, the place of sacrifice, the place of the sanctuary, and a number of other holy things. It is no wonder that the Christians wanted to defend the holy city unto death. They were conditioned to believe that martyrdom in holy war gave them eternal life.

The battle fever was rising high when Saladin gave the command to attack. Then, the fiercest struggle began, and each side fought as an absolute religious obligation. There was no need for a superior authority to urge the soldiers on; each one drove on without being driven back. The slaughter on both sides was heavy and thousands from each army fell in these encounters.

When the Franks saw how violently the Muslims were attacking, their leaders grew desperate and assembled themselves to plan their strategy. They finally decided to surrender and to give Jerusalem over to Saladin. In return, they asked for safe conduct out of the city, but Saladin refused to grant their request, mainly because he wanted to deal with them just as they had dealt with the population of Jerusalem when they conquered it in 1099.

When the Franks lost hope of escape from death, they told Saladin that they would kill their children and wives, burn their possessions, pull down the Sanctuary of the Dome of the Rock and the Masjid al-Aqsa and other sacred places. They also vowed to kill five-thousand Muslim prisoners and then come out and fight with honor unto death. Upon hearing this counteroffer, Saladin granted them safe passage. After the conquest of Jerusalem, Saladin and his followers fell down on their faces and worshipped their God and gave Him thanks for driving His enemies from Jerusalem. The city had been controlled by the Franks for ninety-one years before its recapture by the Muslims.

During the months of April and June of 1191, King Philip II of France, and King Richard the Lion Heart of England arrived in the Holy Land with their mighty armies to fight against the Muslims, who had gradually become weakened, demoralized, lazy, and completely lacking in enthusiasm after their victory at Jerusalem. The crusaders realized that the Muslims had lost their zeal to fight and they began a great offensive. Saladin mounted his horse and ordered his army to attack the enemy. A great battle was fought that day— July 12, 1191; the crusaders won the battle and massacred thousands of Muslims.

The crusaders were able to maintain control of Jerusalem and to dominate strategic passes between the Mediterranean Sea and the Orantes River by building strong castles. Those fortresses were built to protect the coastal cities and the countryside from the unending series of counterattacks by the Muslim armies. Even today, crusader fortresses can be seen in the regions of the "Holy Land", southern Turkey, Syria, Lebanon, Jordan, and on the island of Cyprus.

The strongest and most beautiful castle was called, the *Krak des Chevaliers*, or "Castle of the Knights." It dominated a strategic pass between the Mediterranean and the Syrian cities of Homs and Hama, which are located on the Orantes River. The Arabs called it *Husn al-Akrad*, or "Fortress of the Kurds." The Krak was erected on the foundations of an earlier castle built by the Muslims. T. E. Lawrence called it "perhaps the most wholly admirable castle in the world."

Although the crusader castles were built to serve as defensive retreats, the besieging Muslim forces under the leadership of Salah al-Deen (Saladin) were able to outfox the crusaders by cutting off the source of drinking water and by hurling on them large stone balls. Through such devices, many crusader fortresses, seemingly impregnable, fell to Saladin's ingenuity.

There were many more battles that took place on the "Holy Land" between the Christians and the Muslims. By this time the holy war tradition had become well entrenched.

Contemporary Politics and Conflicts

In the Gulf War (Desert Storm) Saddam Hussein was portrayed as a threat to the free world, with his huge army, his chemical, biological, and potential nuclear weapons, and his crimes against humanity; yet most people have little historical knowledge about Western interferences in the Middle East.

The modern nations of Iraq, Kuwait, Jordan, Lebanon, Syria, Saudi Arabia, and Israel had their borders drawn mainly by the British, with a little help from the French and a few Arab leaders. The borders of Iraq, Kuwait, and Saudi Arabia were drawn by Sir Percy Cox, the British high commissioner for Iraq in 1922. Some territories, such as the present Kingdom of Jordan, had never existed as nations. Others, such as Syria and Iraq, were on the site of ancient nations dating back to the dawn of human history.

Iraq is the site of the ancient civilizations of Babylon, Sumeria, and Mesopotamia. These great civilizations were the first to engage in agriculture and were credited with the development of writing and using the wheel for ground transportation. Hammurabi, king of Babylon, gave the world its first written legal code.

From the fifteenth through the nineteenth centuries, the Middle East was dominated by the Ottoman Empire (modern Turkey). Kuwait was part of the Ottoman province, which was ruled from Istanbul but administered from Basra, Iraq.

Britain controlled many countries and established many colonies by using various kinds of political maneuvering and devious means. For instance, during the nineteenth century, Britain was able to establish influence in the Persian Gulf, which was an important trade route between Europe and India. During that time, the Sabbah family was governing Kuwait, which was then a British colony.

In 1899 the Emirate family signed an agreement to become a British protectorate, but Kuwait remained under Ottoman control until the beginning of World War I. During the war, Britain recruited an influential Arab tribe, called the Hashemites and encouraged them to rebel against Ottoman rule (a version of the story was told in the Hollywood film, *Lawrence of Arabia*). The Hashemites were from Mecca, Saudi Arabia, and were descended from prophet Muhammad.

During the early twentieth century, the British made some promises to the Arabs they did not intend to keep. Those promises were made to the Hashemite leader Sharif Hussein by Sir Henry McMahon, the British high commissioner in Egypt. Sharif Hussein was assured that after the war with Turkey, the Arab portions of the Ottoman Empire would be totally under Hashemite leadership.

After the defeat of Turkey in World War I, Britain broke that promise and took control of Egypt, Iraq, Kuwait, Transjordan (presently the Kingdom of Jordan), and Palestine (now Israel and the occupied territories). Then, Britain gave Lebanon and Syria to France. The French (mostly Catholic by birth) allowed the Lebanese Catholic minority to have the upper hand over the Muslim majority. The decision to make Lebanon a nation in which Muslims would be governed by a Catholic minority led to the civil war that has practically destroyed Lebanon.

In 1917 the British also made promises to the Zionist that Palestine would become an independent Jewish national home. This was known as the Balfour declaration. This kind of subtle political maneuvering by the Western Allies set the Middle East on a course of chronic hostility and bloody wars.

Most Arabs derive part of their anti-British attitudes and anti-American feelings from past exploitations. To Western ears, the Arabs seem to be paranoid when they contend that the West intentionally created the new Arab nations and Israel for their own interests. Winston Churchill, who was colonial secretary of the British Empire at that time, once boasted, "I created Jordan with the stroke of my pen."

Conversely, the British tried to pacify the Arabs by setting up two of Sharif Hussein's sons as kings. Abdullah became king of Transjordan, and Faisal was made king of

Syria. But the French ousted Faisal from Syria, and the British transferred him to the throne of Iraq. The present king of Jordan is Abdullah's grandson.

Western powers have kept the Arab world unstable for an excuse to intervene by claiming to restore stability. History teaches that strong nations have no need for aggressive power, but weak nations are destroyed by it. In other words, nations remain strong when they become champions of peace and human rights.

A case in point about peace and human rights is the foreign policy of former President Jimmy Carter, who was portrayed as a weak leader for concentrating on those issues. Now he has been touted by many as one of the better presidents of the USA. In contrast, George Bush was defeated in the 1992 election after winning a war against Saddam Hussein. Who was the weakest of the two presidents?

The Zionist Massacres

The Jews were also guilty of fighting their holy wars on the Promised Land from the time of their return from exile in Babylon through the period of the Maccabees until the destruction of Jerusalem by the Romans in A.D. 70. The Jewish holy wars began again in 1948. In addition to their national holy wars, the Jews also shed the blood of their own prophets in the "Holy Land". The Lord Jesus said;

> I will send them prophets and apostles, and some of them they will kill and persecute, that the blood of all the prophets which was shed from the foundation of the world may be required of this generation. . . . Yes, I say to you, it shall be required of this generation. (Luke 11:49–51)

78

God held the Jewish nation more accountable than all other nations for rejecting the Messiah. The reason is that unto the Jews "were committed the oracles of God" (Rom. 3:2). The Jews saw how God parted the Red Sea and the Jordan River and witnessed many more miracles of God's saving power. God's judgement finally came as the temple was completely destroyed along with most of Jerusalem in the year 70 A.D. In the following years a temple to Jupiter was erected and the Jews were banned form entering the city for hundreds of years.

The once-oppressed Jews have been replaced by the wandering Palestinians. The Jews, who had been killed and persecuted for nearly a thousand years by Christendom in the West, have now made many enemies in the East by killing and persecuting the Palestinians in their own lands. European Zionists committed many terrorist acts against the helpless old women and children in Palestine (modern Israel). Jacques de Reynir of the International Red Cross reported the inhumane acts of Israelis against the Palestinians on April 13–16, 1948. These reports contain the interrogations of the massacre's survivors and other witnesses by a team of British officers. These interviews were documented by Richard C. Cathing, who was a British assistant inspector general of the Criminal Investigation Division. These atrocities were recorded in a dossier, number: 179/110/17/GS.

The report described in minute detail how the Zionists took many young schoolgirls and raped them and then raped their mothers and later slaughtered all of them. A number of infants were butchered, and old people were killed. Women had their bracelets torn from their arms and their rings from their fingers; sometimes their ears were severed in order to remove their earrings. These animalistic acts by the "chosen people of God" took place in the Palestinian town of Dar Yassin. This habit of making enemies in the name of God has been passed on from one generation to another, and it has "given great occasion to the enemies of the Lord to blaspheme" against Him (2 Sam. 12:14)!

79

Man's Barbaric Nature

It has been said that man has evolved from the animal kingdom, namely the monkey. Occasionally, man may look and act like a monkey, but the main difference is that the monkey possesses a soul, not a spirit. His soul perishes with his animal body. On the other hand, man's soul is indivisibly identified with his human spirit and is, given by this fact, an undying quality. The human soul identified with the human spirit survives the disintegration of the body to remain forever morally responsible to God. If redeemed, it will be eternally united with Christ and numbered with those who have been reconciled to God and "justified by [Christ's] blood" (Rom. 5:9–10); otherwise it will be judged and eternally punished in hell.

Animals usually kill to eat, but man kills for many other reasons, and whatever he touches he corrupts. The reason for this is that he has inherited the Adamic sin nature. The Bible teaches that man's inhumanity to man started when "Cain rose against Abel his brother and killed him" (Gen. 4:8). Since then, man's feet were swift to shed blood and commit other violent crimes against his fellowman.

Throughout history, the grim reality of war has been a horror to behold. Myriads of human beings have died in wars as a result of selfish economic and political reasons. Ironically, man constitutes his own greatest problem. On the one hand, he is capable of reason and compassion possessing both logic and imagination. On the other hand, he is also capable of mercilessly destroying with a cruelty and deliberation unknown to animals.

There exists a conflict between God's infinite wisdom and man's empirical and analytical mind. The Scripture says:

> For it is written: "I will destroy the wisdom of the wise,
> And bring to nothing the understanding of the prudent."
> (1 Cor. 1:19; cf. Isa. 29:14)

Some believe that man has an inborn potential to be a good person, but the prophet Jeremiah cried out:

> The heart is deceitful above all things, And desperately wicked; Who can know it? (Jer. 17:9)

And the apostle Paul reiterated what was said in Psalm 14:3:

There is none who does good, no, not one. (Rom. 3:12)

Secular education is built upon a philosophy that man is basically good. In *The Suicide of the West,* James Burnham noted that this philosophy of man's goodness overlooks entirely certain facts—that Germany produced a Hitler and a Himmler and that Joseph Goebbels had a doctorate in philosophy. Burnham has contended that "highly educated people have inward drives, greeds, compulsions, passions, and a lust for power that are not eliminated by any known process of education." This does not mean that education is evil. Paul was highly educated. Education is good only if it is God centered. The Bible views ignorance as sin and encourages us to learn about how to live with our fellowmen in peace through our Lord Jesus Christ. God said, "My people are destroyed for lack of knowledge" (Hos. 4:6).

Man will never be able to solve the problem of his sin nature by acting independently from his Creator. In fact, man will do well to ponder the promises of the Lord Jesus concerning eternal life. Jesus said, "Most assuredly, I say to you, he who believes in Me has everlasting life" (John 6:47)! In other words, the Christians who are waiting for the "glorious appearing of our great God and Savior Jesus Christ" (Titus 2:13) must strive to become peacemakers, not warmongers!

To the Christian is extended the gracious invitation by the Lord Jesus to "speak the truth in love." So the followers of Christ are to extend peacemaking love to the enemies of Christ, but distortion of the truth can never be one of our tools of peacemaking. An alliance for the sake of the gospel may really be an unholy union. Such unions damage the prospects of peace with God for many Middle Eastern people— both Arabs and Jews.

Understanding Holy Wars
Each of the three monotheistic religions has been trying for centuries to purify the "Holy Land" of all impure races. In

the process of liberating Palestine of all impure races in the name of God, millions have been killed, and most of them were civilians. This habit of fighting under the guise of religion is as old as the Old Testament.

Jews, Christians, and Muslims are all peoples of the Book. They share a common monotheistic belief in one divine God. They share many key values in common: respect for justice, for life, for knowledge, for compassion toward the poor, respect for parents, and the importance of family life. And yet, all three religions have had centuries marked by mutual hostility that has given rise to an enduring tradition of distrust and fear.

To Westerners, the two hundred years of the Crusades are traditionally seen as a series of heroic, chivalrous exploits in which the knights, kings, princes, and peoples of Europe tried to wrest Jerusalem from the "wicked Muslim infidels."

To Muslims, the Crusades were an episode of great cruelty and terrible plunder by European "infidels" and peoples of fortune. To Westerners, 1492 memorializes the great accomplishments of Columbus and the discovery of the Americas. To Muslims, 1492 is a year of tragedy when Granada fell to Ferdinand and Isabella, putting an end to eight centuries of Muslim civilization in Europe. For the Jews, who made great contributions to Spanish culture, 1492 marks the year they were forced out of Spain.

God's Judgment on Holy Warriors

The three monotheistic religions, which have been fighting their holy wars in the name of God, have earned the title as "enemies of God," and they will be "judged according to their works" (Rev. 20:12). There is nothing holy in killing a human being who was created in the image of God (Gen. 1:27). In fact, God said that "Whoever sheds man's blood, by man his blood shall be shed; For in the image of God He made man" (Gen. 9:6). Man is still the image bearer of God in many respects. We have the ability to communicate, to love, to bear moral responsibility, to work, and we are in physical bodies like the Lord Jesus had. In this sense, man is created in the image of God. However, only God is holy, and the day will come when He will plead His holy cause against those who disobey Him, "because He has appointed a day on which He will judge the world in righteousness by the Man [Jesus] whom He has ordained. He has given assurance of this to all by raising Him from the dead" (Acts 17:31).

The resurrection of the Lord Jesus from the dead in a physical body gives to the elect the assurance that He is God and that He is man. Because He is man, He has the right to judge men. The Lord Jesus is acquainted with all the weaknesses of earthly existence, yet He went through tremendous tests to His body and soul without sin. It is this One who has the absolute right to rule and to judge the world (John 5:21–29).

Countless believers have faced death for taking an uncompromising stand for their faith in Jesus Christ. They have been thrown to the lions, stoned to death, crucified, sawn in two, beheaded, burned at the stake, and imprisoned. Such persons were individuals "of whom the world was not worthy" (Heb. 11:36–38). They did not die fighting a holy war or suffering for any evil deed they had done. Their death was a holy death, their cause a holy cause!

HOLY DEATH

Saladin was a great hero of holy wars, but many Arabs and others who were martyred for their uncompromising faith in Christ are much greater heroes than Saladin in the eyes of God. One such hero of the faith was a Lebanese who was called "the Paul of the Arab world." Following is his story as it was told to me during my visit to Lebanon in 1968–70.

Asa'ad Shidyak was born to a Lebanese Catholic family. His parents trained him according to their ethnic conditioning and encouraged him to study for the priesthood. After he completed his education, he entered a monastery and lived an ascetic and celibate life and became devoutly attentive to the rigid discipline of the priesthood. He began an intensive study of Scripture and was aware of the spiritual laxity in high ecclesiastical places. For Asa'ad those years were times of profound physical and spiritual torment.

After studying diligently Paul's letter to the Galatians, he became obsessed with anxieties about his own salvation. In spite of seeking relief in frequent confessions and extreme asceticism, his search for peace of mind led him to a further understanding of the doctrine of soteriology (salvation). He discovered the free gift of salvation through faith alone in Christ Jesus.

As a consequence of his newly found faith and convictions, he felt compelled to protest against many of the doctrines of the Catholic Church, as Martin Luther had done before him. For example, Asa'ad denied the authority of the priest to forgive sin and emphasized the doctrine of justification by faith alone. His uncompromising stand in doctrinal matters gave his opponents the opportunity to condemn his views as heretical and to banish him.

He was given ample time to recant, but he stood firm on his convictions. He was then coerced into entering an uninhabited and isolated convent and was forced to stand in a narrow hole where a rope was put around his neck. Day after day a priest came by and pulled the rope hard in an attempt to persuade Asa'ad to recant. Finally, because of Asa'ad's stubborn refusal to change his mind, he was hanged!

A Palestinian missionary, whom I met in Europe in 1994, shared with me the story of another hero of the faith.

As the Gulf War of 1991 came to an end, the Palestinian missionary was able to rush to Iraq in order to try to evangelize some Muslims. While in Baghdad he befriended a devout Sunni Muslim by the name of Suleiman. After a few encounters with the missionary, the Lord opened Suleiman's heart to heed the things spoken to him concerning the doctrine of salvation through faith in Christ. Suleiman believed and became a bold witness for his Lord and Savior Jesus Christ.

However, the news of Suleiman's conversion reached the ears of his relatives. As a result, the temperature of their smoldering anger rapidly mounted until their uncontrollable rage was set ablaze. They took Suleiman to a public place and beat him until one of his cousins shot him to death.

The Lord Jesus said, "And do not fear those who kill the body but cannot kill the soul. But rather fear Him who is able to destroy both soul and body in hell" (Matt. 10:28).

There are many other Muslim converts who are being martyred for their faith in Christ whose names are not known in the West. The reason that Arab converts are still dying for their faith in Christ is that Jesus is hated by the unbelieving world. Jesus said:

If the world hates you, you know that it hated Me before it hated you. . . . He who hates Me hates My Father also. (John 15:18–23)

John the Discipler

John the Beloved was the only apostle whom the Lord spared from martyrdom. The reason seems to be that God wanted him to write the Book of the Revelation of Jesus Christ. In addition to writing the last book of the Bible and to mentoring many saints, John was able to influence two notable bishops who became examples of walking "in the truth" (3 John 3), which culminated in their martyrdom.[1] These two men were Ignatius and Polycarp.

The paramount era of holy death or Christian martyrdom was the first three centuries of the Christian epoch. The term martyr comes from the Greek word *martys,* which means "witness." In the second century it began to be used to designate a believer who suffered and died for his faith. After death the martyr was called a confessor of the faith. No doubt, the spectacle of martyrdom was quite soul-stirring and faith-strengthening. The confidence and boldness of the martyrs became a witness to the reality of Christ's resurrection and His conquest of death and hell. In monastic circles, martyrdom began to have a spiritual interpretation, which was that the martyrs were bearers of the Holy Spirit in a special way. This would be an easy conclusion to make because the martyrs had visions; they did miracles by the touch of their own bodies; and they repelled demonic powers. It was even believed by some that martyrdom had propitiatory value, in which the whole community of faith shared in the benefits of grace that God had bestowed on the witness.[2]

Ignatius

Ignatius, who followed the Lord in holy death, was the Syrian Bishop of Antioch. His death preceded that of Polycarp, occurring in the reign of Trajan (98-117A.D.).[3] Ignatius, called *Theophorus* or the "God bearer", succeeded Evodius as bishop and served in that office for forty years.

On his way to Rome to be martyred by wild beasts in the amphitheater, he wrote important letters to the churches in Rome and in Asia Minor. He also wrote an encouraging letter to Polycarp. These letters were invaluable testimony of uncompromising faith to the early Christians. In one of his letters, he said:

> From Syria even unto Rome I fight with wild beasts, by land and sea, by night and by day, being bound amidst ten leopards, even a company of soldiers, who only wax worse when they are kindly treated.[4]

As he travel to Rome, he stopped and preached in Philadelphia, then he reached Smyrna where he visited with bishop Polycarp. While there he received visits from the bishops of Ephesus, Tralles, and Magnesia. Ignatius then gave each of them a letter for their churches; he also wrote a letter to the Romans. He then went to Troas where he wrote letters to Philadelphia and Smyrna and a personal letter to Polycarp. In these letters Ignatius stressed the virgin birth, the doctrine of Christ, and the spiritual mystery of the Trinity. These seven letters form a dossier that was widely circulated in the early church.[5] These letters present to us the aroma of the fragrance of Christ, as well as giving us a picture of early church life. Ignatius' epistles breathe an apostolic spirit and a familiarity with still-living Bible characters such as Onesimus. In his letter to the Ephesians, Ignatius states:

> for when ye heard that I was on my way from Syria, in bonds for the sake of the common Name and hope, and was hoping through your prayers to succeed in fighting with wild beasts in Rome, that by so succeeding I might have power to be a disciple, ye were eager to visit me: seeing then that in God's name I have received your whole multitude in the person of Onesimus, whose love passeth utterance and who is moreover your bishop . . . I pray that you may love him according to Jesus Christ and that ye all may be like him; for blessed is He that granted unto you according to your deserving to have such a bishop.[6]

It seems impossible now to recover the white heat of early church fathers like Ignatius in following the Lord in holy death. We can only read and marvel. In this selection from his letter to the Romans, Ignatius develops his theology of martyrdom.

> Let me be given to the wild beasts, for through them I can attain unto God. I am God's wheat, and I am ground by the teeth of wild beasts that I may be found pure bread (of Christ). Rather entice the wild beasts, that they may become my sepulchre and may leave no part of my body behind, so that I may not, when I am fallen asleep, be burdensome to any one. Then shall I be truly a disciple of Jesus Christ, when the world shall not so much as see my body. . . . If I shall suffer, then am I a freed-man of Jesus Christ, and I shall rise free in Him.[7]

Upon his initial arrest and cross-examination by the emperor Trajan, Ignatius makes his typical good confession of faith:

> TRAJAN: Who are you, spirit of evil, who dare to disobey my orders and who goad others on to their destruction?
>
> IGNATIUS: No one calls Theophorus "spirit of evil."
>
> TRAJAN: Who is Theophorus?
>
> IGNATIUS: He who bears Christ within him.
>
> TRAJAN: And do not we bear within ourselves those gods who help us against our enemies?
>
> IGNATIUS: You are mistaken when you call gods those who are no better than devils. For there is only one God who made heaven and earth and all that is in them: and one Jesus Christ into whose kingdom I earnestly desire to be admitted.

TRAJAN: Do you mean Him who was crucified under Pontius Pilate?

IGNATIUS: Yes, the same who by His death has crucified both sin and its author, and has proclaimed that every malice of the devil should be trodden under foot by those who bear Him in their hearts.

TRAJAN: Do you then carry about Christ within you?

IGNATIUS: Yes, for it is written, I will dwell in them and will walk with them.

When Trajan gave sentence that the bishop should be bound and taken to Rome to be devoured by the wild beasts for the pleasure and entertainment of the people, the saint exclaimed through rapturous prayer, "I thank Thee, O Lord, for putting within my reach this pledge of perfect love for Thee, and for allowing me to be bound for Thy sake with chains, after the example of Thy apostle Paul."[8]

Polycarp

The biblical prediction of martyrdom is given particularly to the church at Smyrna located in present-day Turkey. *Smyrna* comes from the Greek word meaning "myrrh." This aromatic resin, when crushed, emits a wonderful fragrance. In the letter to the Smyrnean church in Revelation, it is evident that the church is to undergo persecution that will no doubt produce the fragrance of Christ. ". . . You will have tribulation ten days. Be faithful until death, and I will give you the crown of life" (Rev. 2:10). It is out of the experiences of this church that we have the story of Polycarp, who was martyred in 155.

Polycarp was a highly respected man of God, who lived to an advanced age.[9] He was kindly and grave in demeanor, but spoke with boldness when the occasion demanded it. Marcion, an early heretic, who taught the existence of two gods as father and son, was met on the street by Polycarp one day.

Marcion said, "Acknowledge us," as if to say, "Salute us." Polycarp replied: "I acknowledge the firstborn of Satan."

The church at Smyrna preserves for us, in a letter, the circumstances surrounding the death of Polycarp and the general climate of persecution against the church. This letter is addressed from the church at Smyrna to the church at Philomelium. The general conditions of persecution are as follows:

> Blessed therefore and noble are all the martyrdoms which have taken place according to the will of God. . . . For who could fail to admire their nobleness and patient endurance and loyalty to the Master? Seeing that when they were so torn by lashes that the mechanism of their flesh was visible even as far as the inward veins and arteries, they endured patiently, so that the very bystanders had pity and wept; while they themselves reached such a pitch of bravery that none of them uttered a cry or a groan, thus showing to us all that at that hour the martyrs of Christ being tortured were absent from the flesh, or rather that the Lord was standing by and conversing with them. . . . And in like manner also those that were condemned to the wild beasts endured fearful punishments, being made to lie on sharp shells and buffeted with other forms of manifold tortures, that the devil might, if possible, by the persistence of the punishment bring them to a denial; for he tried many wiles against them.[10]

After the death of a certain glorious martyr named Germanicus, the crowd became incensed against Polycarp and demanded that he be sought and punished. Polycarp was urged by his parishioners to escape from the city. This he did, and escaped to a nearby farm. While at the farm, Polycarp had a dream in which his pillow seemed to be consumed by flames, which Polycarp interpreted as meaning he would have to suffer for Christ by burning. However, his friends continued to encourage him to flee into another part of the country. In this second retreat his adversaries found him. Polycarp's response was "the Lord's will be done." He greeted his pursuers with cheerfulness and kindness and ordered a refreshing meal to be prepared for them. He requested only that he be given an hour to pray. The unction the Lord gave him in prayer served to smite his pursuers to the quick.

His adversaries conducted him into the city riding on a donkey. At which time a certain official named Herod tried to persuade him to preserve his life by saying; "What harm is there in saying Lord Caesar and to sacrifice, and thus save your life?" Polycarp of course refused. Although having sprained his thigh, he continued eagerly (limping into the stadium). He heard a voice from heaven saying; "Be strong, Polycarp, and contend manfully." Again the officials tried to convince Polycarp to preserve his life by reviling Christ. Polycarp replied, "Eighty and six years have I served Him, and He never did me wrong. How can I now blaspheme my King who has saved me?"

The proconsul desired Polycarp to justify himself before the people. To which Polycarp replied:

> I have thought proper to give you a reason; for we have been taught to give magistrates and powers appointed by God the honour that is due to them, as far as it does not injure us; but I do not consider those the proper ones before whom I should deliver my defence. The proconsul said, "I have wild beasts at hand; I will cast you to these unless you change your mind." He answered, "Call them. For we have no reason to repent from the better to the worse, but it is good to change from wickedness to virtue." He again urged him. "I will cause you to be consumed by fire, should you despise the beasts, and not change your mind." Polycarp answered "You threaten fire that burns for a moment and is soon extinguished, for you know nothing of the judgment to come, and the fire of eternal punishment reserved for the wicked. But why do you delay? Bring what you wish."[11]

The multitude cried for his death by burning, and the pile was quickly prepared. The executioners were preparing to secure him to the stake with spikes, but Polycarp asked to be allowed to stand freely. So he was merely bound to the stake. At that time, Polycarp uttered his prayer, which began thus:

> Father of thy well-beloved and blessed Son Jesus Christ, through whom we have received the knowledge of thee. The God of angels and powers, and all creation, and of all the family of the righteous, that live before thee, I bless thee that thou hast thought me worthy of the present day and hour, to have a share in the number of the martyrs and in the cup of Christ, unto the resurrection of eternal life, both of the soul and body, in the incorruptible felicity of the Holy Spirit.[12]

The flames were immediately kindled and arose to great height and enclosed Polycarp in something like an oven, but he was not consumed. The believers perceived a fragrant odor like myrrh or other incense. The executioner was forced to plunge a sword into him, and a great quantity of blood gushed out extinguishing the flames. The body was then burned by the executioners until nothing was left but the bones. However, the story of this great apostolic father still persists until today.

Justin Martyr

Another Middle-Eastern martyr was the apostolic father who also bore the name martyr. Justin Martyr was born in Flavia Neapolis (Nablus near ancient Sichem). His parents were thought to be Greeks, but by place of birth and culture, Justin was a Palestinian Samaritan. He was put to death during the reign of Marcus Aurelius in A.D. 165.

Justin was a second-century philosopher and apologist for the Christian faith. He was one of the first Christians to use philosophical terms in explaining the Christian faith. He loved to speak of God's creative and saving plan that was manifested and fulfilled by Christ the Logos. The scope of Justin's theology and teaching was truly massive.

He attributed Old Testament theophanies to the Logos "in human form," and he saw clearly that Messiah, the Word, was found in the Law and the Prophets. The priesthood of all believers was taught by him, as well as the reality of exorcism and the role of Satan in this world.

Justin had a well-developed eschatology. All human history is oriented toward the Second Coming of Christ. First comes the resurrection of the saints; . . . finally the resurrection of the wicked will be accomplished followed by final judgment.[13]

Justin was converted to Christ around the age of thirty. He had studied philosophy and was well-versed in the various schools of thought. One day, as he was walking by the seashore, perhaps near Ephesus, he observed that he was being followed by an old man. He stopped, greeted him, and began a conversation with him about the search for truth. The old man kindly unfolded to him the fact that there was a more noble and satisfying philosophy than any he had yet studied and that it had been initially revealed to the Hebrew prophets of old. Hebrew prophecy had reached its consummation in Jesus Christ. The old stranger urged Justin to pray fervently that the doors of light might be opened to allow him to obtain the knowledge God alone can give. This conversation gave Justin the desire to study Scripture. He embraced the faith shortly after that.[14]

In Rome, Justin publicly debated with a Cynic philosopher named Crescens. Justin defeated him and exposed him as an ignorant man and a liar; he also made a great enemy for himself. It is believed that through the machinations of Crescens, Justin was arrested on a second visit to Rome. Justin was beheaded along with six other martyrs. He was tried before the Roman Prefect Rusticus, where he made a good confession for Christ:

RUSTICUS: What branch of learning do you study?
JUSTIN: I have studied all in turn. But I finished by deciding on the Christian teaching, however disagreeable it may be to those who are deceived by error.
RUSTICUS: And that is the learning you love, you foolish man?

Justin: Yes. I follow the Christians because they have the truth.

Rusticus: What is this teaching?

Justin: We believe in the one creator God, and confess His Son, Jesus Christ, of whom the prophets spoke, the bringer of salvation and judge of mankind.

Rusticus: Where do the Christian assemblies take place?

Justin: Wherever they can. Do you suppose we all meet in the same place? Not a bit of it. The God of the Christians is not found in any particular place. He is invisible, He is everywhere in heaven and earth, and His faithful ones praise and worship Him everywhere and anywhere.

Rusticus: All right then, tell me where you foregather with your followers.

Justin: I have always stayed at the house of a man called Martin, just by Timothy's baths. This is the second time I have been in Rome, and I have never stayed anywhere else. Anybody who wants to can find me and hear the true doctrine there.

Rusticus: You, then, are a Christian?

Justin: Yes, I am a Christian.

Rusticus: Listen, you who are said to be eloquent and who believe you have the truth—if I have you beaten and be-headed, do you believe that you will then go to heaven?"

Justin: If I suffer as you say, I hope to receive the reward of those who keep Christ's commandments. I know that all who do that, will remain in God's grace even to the consummation of all things.

Rusticus: So you think that you will go up to heaven, there to receive a reward?

Justin: I don't think it, I know it. I have no doubt about it whatever.

Rusticus: Very well. Come here and sacrifice to the gods.

Justin: Nobody in his senses gives up truth for falsehood.

Rusticus: If you don't do as I tell you, you will be tortured without mercy.

Justin: We ask nothing better than to suffer for the sake of our Lord Jesus Christ and so to be saved. If we do this we can stand confidently and quietly before the fearful judge-ment seat of that same God and Savior, when in accor-dance with divine ordering, all this world will pass away.

Justin's fellow martyrs agreed with him, and they were then scourged and beheaded. They fulfilled their final witness to Christ in the common place of execution. Their brethren secretly bore their bodies away and buried them in a fitting place.[15]

The Reason for Persecution

Servants of Christ have always been persecuted by those who hate the claims of the Lord Jesus, mainly because He declared that He is God in the flesh. According to the writings of the apostles, persecution of the Christians is an outgrowth of the world's hatred of Christ. The Lord Jesus Himself said to His disciples, "Blessed are you when they revile and persecute you, and say all kinds of evil against you falsely for my sake . . . . And you will be hated by all for my name's sake. But he who endures to the end will be saved" (Matt. 5:11, 10:22; cf. John 15:18).

Dioko is a Greek term meaning "to pursue, to persecute or to run after." It is used more than thirty times in the New Testament. Based on the writings of the church fathers, such as Tertullian and Justin Martyr, persecution is the appointment of God for the trial of faith and for conforming the saints ". . . to the image of His Son. . . ." (Rom. 8:29).

Tertullian believed that persecution is a means by which a Christian is declared either approved or rejected in the just judgment of God. Justin Martyr described persecution as the fan that cleanses the Lord's threshing floor, the church, separating the grains of the martyrs from the chaff of the deniers. Both Tertullian and Justin Martyr agreed that through persecution, God's glory is revealed in the face of His servants' weakness; it reinforces their trust in Him and revives them spiritually.

I cannot cease from marvelling at those who have fought and are still fighting their holy wars, and at those who have died and are still dying a holy death for their faith in Christ. Dying in a holy war does not secure eternal salvation, but being persecuted for the sake of Christ will surely lead to a glorious reunion with Him in heaven. Contrary to what the world teaches, true Christianity does not promote holy wars, nor does it endorse coercive exploitation and usurpation of other nations, but it does encourage the faithful believers in Christ to endure suffering for His sake, even "until death!" (Rev. 2:10).

> Who shall separate us from the love of Christ? Shall tribulation, or distress, or persecution, or famine, or nakedness, or peril, or sword? As it is written: 'For Your sake we are killed all day long; We are accounted as sheep for the slaughter.' Yet in all these things we are more than conquerors through Him who loved us. For I am persuaded that neither death nor life, nor angels nor principalities nor powers, nor things present nor things to come, nor height nor depth, nor any other created thing, shall be able to separate us from the love of God which is in Christ Jesus our Lord. (Rom. 8:35–39)

HOLY ALLIANCE

The Old Testament contains several prophecies about judgment on the Arab world, but it also contains many exciting promises of blessings upon the Arabs.[1] Perhaps, the most important promise of blessing is found in Isaiah 19.

According to Isaiah, God has predetermined to save a remnant of Arabs and Jews and to initiate a holy alliance between them. The holy alliance will take place during the millennial reign of Christ on the earth, and not before. Isaiah predicted

> there will be an altar to the Lord in the midst of the land of Egypt, and a pillar to the Lord at its border. And it will be for a sign and for a witness to the Lord of hosts in the land of Egypt; for they will cry to the Lord because of the oppressors, and He will send them a Savior and a Mighty One [the Lord Jesus Christ], and He will deliver them. Then the Lord will be known to Egypt, and the Egyptians will know the Lord in that day. . . . In that day Israel will be one of three with Egypt and Assyria [modern Iraq] . . . Whom the Lord of hosts shall bless, saying, "Blessed is Egypt My people, and Assyria the work of My hands, and Israel My inheritance." (Isa. 19:19–25)

The words that day refer to the millennium. When Isaiah says that God "will send them a Savior and a Mighty One," he is predicting the Second Coming of Christ to rule the nations of the world during the millennium.

The word *millennium* is not found in the Bible. It is composed of two Latin words: *mille*, meaning "a thousand," and *annum*, meaning "year or years." The New Testament is written in the Greek language, and the Greek words, *chilia etee*, are translated in the English versions, "a thousand years" (Rev. 20:2–7).

Recent History of the Alliance

Israel became a nation in 1948. Since that time, much effort has been exerted to reach out for peace and to gain direct channels of dialogue between the state of Israel and its Arab neighbors. Recent history shows that attempts are underway to form an alliance between Israel and Arab countries.

Egypt was the first to negotiate a peaceful solution to the intractable problem with Israel, which led to the 1978 Camp David Accords and the 1979 Egypt-Israel peace treaty. On October 30–November 1, 1991, a conference was convened in Madrid in order to open direct bilateral negotiations between Israel, Jordan, Syria, Lebanon, and the Palestinians. This led to the signing of the Israel-PLO Declaration of Principles in September, 1993, and the subsequent Gaza-Jericho Agreement in May, 1994. Also, Jordan and Israel signed a common agenda in September, 1993, followed by the Washington Declaration in July, 1994.

All these efforts to reach out for peace should be encouraged. Moshe Aumann's of the journal *Christians and Israel* states:

> As believers in God's unchanging Word, we must ask ourselves: Are we entitled to give up portions of the Land of Israel—even for the sake of achieving peace with our Arab neighbors? . . . The Bible gives us at least three different definitions of the Land's dimensions (see Gen. 15:18; Num. 34:1–15; Ezek. 47:15–20). The nation's history has followed these varying delineations of Israel's borders. Only twice . . . did Israel's frontiers extend all the way to the Euphrates River; in other periods, the country was much smaller than that. Is there not a message here? I think the

Bible is telling us that, down through the ages, the size of Israel's patrimony will not be uniform, but will vary with the prevailing social, political and military circumstances. Thus the notion of territorial compromise with the surrounding Arab nations, for the sake of peace, should not be dismissed out of hand.[2]

However, the Bible asks the following pertinent question; "Can two walk together, unless they are agreed?" (Amos 3:3); and how can man live in peace with his fellowman, unless first he can have "peace with God through our Lord Jesus Christ" (Rom. 5:1)? Because salvation is the most important theme in the Bible, it should transcend all personal opinions and theological persuasions. History teaches that the oppressed cannot live in peace with the oppressor. It is one of the great ironies of history that the roots of the present Arab-Jewish struggle should have grown from mistreatment each has received from the other. The Arabs and Jews are Semitic cousins who share cultural traits and traditions but unfortunately were destined to fight for possession of the same territory.

No matter what biblical interpretation has been advanced in support of the State of Israel, the majority of the Palestinians and their counterparts will remain a thorn in the flesh for Israel until the Prince of Peace [the Lord Jesus Christ] returns to Israel to establish a holy alliance between Arabs and Jews during the millennium. The nineteenth chapter of Isaiah describes the fulfillment of this exciting future union.

Historical Background of Isaiah 19

Isaiah, a great prophet of God, was a product of the finest culture of Judah and spoke with the moral authority and boldness that befitted an ambassador of the Almighty. Isaiah was familiar with the way of life of the ruling classes of his time and had easy access to the kings.[3]

Isaiah prophesied in the reigns of four Judean kings—Uzziah, Jotham, Ahaz, and Hezekiah. His early ministry began around the year 742 B.C. This was the time when the Assyrian threat to Israel began to be felt after a long period of relative peace. Tiglath-pileser III invaded northern Israel and required tribute payment. This fact gives the doom like quality to some of Isaiah's prophecies, such as 6:11–13. In the early chapters of the Book of Isaiah, the oracles concerning Judah and Jerusalem deal with religious idolatry, greed, and social injustice of the upper classes in particular.

During the approximate period 734–715 B.C., Isaiah prophesied to Ahaz king of Judah not to appeal to Assyria for help in the war against a coalition of Syria and Israel that had made an alliance to overthrow Judah. Ahaz refused to heed the warning, and Isaiah spoke no more to Ahaz.

After the death of Ahaz, and the accession of Hezekiah to the throne, Isaiah predicted the renewed Assyrian threat— this time not against Israel, but against Judah itself.[4] Sargon II, king of Assyria—the predominant world power—conquered Syria and Lebanon before defeating Israel in 722 B.C., at which time Judah was under the threat of Assyrian conquest.

The sea trade of the eastern Mediterranean was controlled by Judah and several Philistine cities. This lucrative commerce was of interest to Assyria and Egypt. Egypt was the second world power of the day. Therefore, the continuing incursions by Assyria into Judah became a matter of concern for Egypt. In 720 B.C., Sargon attacked Philistia, causing the king of Gaza to appeal to Egypt for aid. Gaza nevertheless fell, and Sargon set up a trading center there, but made no move to invade Egypt.

In 713 B.C., the Egyptians encouraged a revolt by the Philistine city of Ashdod against their Assyrian masters. The king of Ashdod, Yamani, fled to Egypt, but the Egyptians sent him back to the Assyrians, thus maintaining cordial relations.[5]

After the death of Sargon in 705 B.C., Sennacherib, king of Assyria, invaded Judah. Forty-six of King Hezekiah's fortified cities in Judah fell to Sennacherib. Hezekiah appealed to Egypt for help. Isaiah denounced this appeal and encouraged dependence on Yahweh alone. Why depend on a weak reed like Egypt?[6]

An army composed of Egyptians, Cushites, and Libyans met the Assyrians at the battle of Eltekeh (2 Kings 18:13–19:37). The Egyptian forces under Taharqa lost this battle; but the Assyrians failed to take Jerusalem, as Isaiah prophesied. The prophecy of Isaiah 19 comes from this background.

Importance of Egypt

Few civilizations of ancient times surpassed the Egyptians in importance. From the land of the pharaohs came the stimulus for numerous intellectual achievements. Important elements of philosophy, mathematics, science, and literature had their beginnings there.

The Egyptians also developed one of the oldest systems of jurisprudence and political theory. They were among the first peoples to have a clear concept of art, and they originated architectural principles that were destined to be used throughout subsequent history.

The oldest of Egypt's architectural wonders dates back to the periods of the pharaohs (2780–2270 B.C.). This was the epoch of the pyramids: the Step Pyramid, the first pyramid in Egypt; and the three famous pyramids of Giza, built by the Fourth-Dynasty kings: Cheops, Chephren, and Mycerinos. The main significance of the pyramids was political and religious. Their construction was an attempt to endow Egypt with immortality and stability.

In addition to the pyramids, the Temples of Karnak and Luxor and Abu Simbel are the leading architectural wonders. Egyptian temples were characterized by massive size. The Karnak temple is the largest religious edifice ever built. Its central hall alone could contain almost any of the Gothic cathedrals of Europe.[7]

Across from Luxor, on the west bank of the Nile, lies the Valley of the Kings, where many pharaohs and their queens are buried. Among the most notable monuments in the Valley of the Kings is the Temple of Deir-el-Bahari of Queen Hatshepsut; she gave Moses his name and adopted him as her son (See Exod. 2:1–10).

As far back as the time of Plato, the intellects of the world traveled to Egypt to marvel at its cultural institutions and monuments. Since ancient times, travelers and explorers and throngs of tourists have flocked to Egypt to discover for themselves these wonders.

From a biblical point of view, Egypt is given much attention because the fortunes of the Jews have been intertwined with those of Egypt at least three different times: (1) during the days of Abraham; (2) during the days of Jacob and Joseph; and (3) during the early days of the infant Jesus.

It was in Egypt where Abraham and his people found hospitality during the great famine (Gen. 12:10–20). It was in Egypt where the pharaoh gave Joseph an Egyptian wife and made him the second ruler of his land (Gen. 41:40–45). It was in Egypt where Jacob and his children lived "in the best of the land, in the land of Rameses [the land of Goshen], as pharaoh had commanded (Gen. 47:11). It was in Egypt where the children of Israel multiplied and were blessed as "the Lord had given the people favor in the sight of the Egyptians" (Exod. 12:36). And it was in Egypt where the infant Jesus found shelter until the death of King Herod, so that the prophecy might be fulfilled: "Out of Egypt I called My Son" (Matt. 2:15; cf. Hos. 11:1)!

Since the time of Christ, great numbers of Jews settled in Egypt, and Alexandria became predominantly a Jewish city. There the Septuagint translation of the Old Testament from Hebrew to Greek was made by the Jews.

Typology of Egypt

The Bible is replete with symbolism and typology. For instance, God told Abraham that his descendants would become slaves in Egypt (Gen. 15:13). Here Egypt is a picture-prophecy of the slave market, which intimates metaphorically the world system under the leadership of pharaoh, a type of Satan who opposes the chosen people of God. Since mankind is born with the Adamic sin nature, every person who has lived on this earth is born in slavery to sin and the coercive power of this world. The problem is, how can we get out of Egypt? We cannot escape from Egypt without a deliverer. This truth has been illustrated in the book of Exodus through Moses, a type of Christ who delivers His people from their slavery to sin. Exodus helps us understand God's judgment against Egypt in Isaiah 19.

The word *exodus* is derived from the Vulgate, through the Septuagint, meaning "going out" or "departure".[8] The same word is used in Luke 9:31 where our Lord Jesus spoke of His exodus. This is a wonderful spiritual truth concerning our physical death.

When a believer dies he leaves a world of testing, suffering, trial, and all Satanic obstructions. After we die, we enter into the very presence of God and eternal joy. It is only because of what the Lord Jesus Christ has done for us at Calvary that we can look forward to our exodus from this sin-cursed earth.

Exodus is the book of deliverance, in which the doctrine of redemption is prominent. Redemption is used here symbolically in reference to the death of Christ. Theologically the word *redemption* is used to include all that Christ had accomplished by His death on the cross. Redemption is the payment of the price demanded by Almighty God to deliver us from the slavery of sin and to set us free from eternal condemnation.

Redemption is the act of buying a slave out of the slave market so that he or she will never again be brought back within its power. It symbolizes the fact that a slave is able to become a child of God, and the means of this miraculous transfer is the blood of the Passover lamb (Exod. 12:21–23). God's redemption (salvation) is always by blood, the precious blood of the "Lamb of God who takes away the sin of the world" (John 1:29)! By contrast, millions have shed their blood needlessly in pursuit of salvation promised by false prophets and religious leaders, as discussed in the chapter on holy wars.

Without the death of Christ there would be no sacrifice for sin, no salvation, no resurrection and none of the other elements that have formed the content of Christian faith from the beginning. The fact that the Christian church was able to endure centuries of persecution and to survive centuries of neglect and opposition is difficult to explain apart from the system of theology stemming from belief in Jesus Christ as the Son of God who actually died, rose and ascended into heaven.[9]

The book of Exodus begins with the words "Now these are the names of the children of Israel who came to Egypt" (Exod. 1:1). There is a wonderful message in this opening statement: that redemption has to do with names. God has a book called the Lamb's Book of Life. God's book of life is also a book of redemption that may very well begin in the same way: "Now these are the names of the children of God who came to heaven."

It seems that every person who has lived on earth has his or her name written in the book of life. This is similar to the book that was kept of all the children of Israel who were living at any one time. When a person died, his or her name was scratched out or deleted from the book. In a similar fashion, when a person dies and has never been saved, his or her name is blotted out "from the book of life" (Rev. 3:5; cf. Exod. 32:32–33).

Think of what it will be like in the day of the great White Throne Judgment when the book of life is opened and a multitude of names have been blotted out because these persons have lived and died without having been redeemed by the blood of the Lamb (Rev. 20:11–15)!

Along with the children of Israel, many Egyptians believed in the God of Moses and were delivered also out of Egypt. Among them were the two Egyptian midwives. Josephus tells us that the two midwives of Exodus 1:15 were Egyptians,[10] who evidently bore Hebrew names because they were believers in the God of Moses. *Shiphrah* means "splendor, or beauty," and *Puah*, "glitter, or brilliancy."

Josephus recounts another Hebrew story connected with the birth of Moses and the Exodus. It seems that a certain fortune-teller told the pharaoh that a child would be born to the Israelites, who would bring the Egyptians low and would raise the status of the Hebrews. He would be excellent in virtue and obtain glory that would be remembered to the end of time. Hearing this, the king became fearful for his throne and ordered every male child to be cast into the river and destroyed. The midwives also were ordered to watch the labors of the Hebrew women to see if male or female children were born. The male children were to be killed.[11] It was at this point that the faith of the Egyptian midwives became paramount. It is interesting to see here how God used the Egyptian believers to protect the Hebrew children from being killed. One of those children became known as Moses.

Contrary to Pharaoh's commandment, the Egyptian midwives feared God and saved the male children (Exod. 1:17). The Lord blessed them for their faith and obedience by giving them husbands and children (Exod. 1:21).

Prophecies against Egypt

At the time of Isaiah's prophecy (742-701 B.C.), the Egyptians had prided themselves on having a mighty army and on being the most learned and wise people on earth. Yet, they were immersed in worshiping a conglomeration of deities; most of them were animals—principally the bull, the cat, the cow, the crocodile, and so forth. The Nile also was important in Egypt's system of idolatrous veneration. Apparently the Egyptians did not learn from the Exodus how God dealt with their idolatry during the time of Moses. The Lord punished Egypt by sending ten plagues on the land to demonstrate His power over idolatry. In Isaiah 19, God inflicted Egypt with similar plagues.

The Egyptians had many gods, and in the ancient world the name of a deity told about that deity. One of the deities was the Nile river. The Nile was worshipped because it gave life to Egypt. The Nile was Egypt's patron god. Through the process of irrigation, the Egyptians were able to produce crops for their livelihood. Bathing in the Nile was, as the Ganges is today in India, a great religious ceremony of purification.

The Egyptians had a frog-headed goddess named Hekt. This goddess was believed to have the power of creation. The Egyptians did not kill frogs; they worshipped them.

Apis the bull was one of the most sacred animals in Egypt. Besides Apis, there was Mnevis the cow; Khum the ram; and the goddess Hathor, which was cowheaded. All of these animals were worshipped by the Egyptians.

The highest deity in Egypt was Ra, the sun god. *The Pharaoh* means *phra*, "the sun." In Exodus 9:17 we notice that Pharaoh is said to have exalted himself. In that, he portrays the antichrist, "who opposes and exalts himself above all that is called God . . . showing himself that he is God" (2 Thess. 2:4).

For that reason, God sent darkness over Egypt for three days, because only God is light and in Him is no darkness. Darkness shows the absence of God. That judgment reveals Egypt was, for the time being, abandoned by God, and nothing remains but death (Exod. 10:21–29; cf. Rev. 16:10). Likewise, God is planning to treat Egypt during the Great Tribulation as He did at the Exodus, as it was predicted in Isaiah 19:1–15.

It is important at this juncture to note that plagues similar to those of Exodus and Isaiah 19 will be repeated with more severity in the Great Tribulation, as predicted by the Lord Jesus in Matthew 24:21:

> For then there will be great tribulation, such as has not been since the beginning of the world until this time, no, nor ever shall be.

The conflict between Moses and Pharaoh was merely a foreshadowing of the conflict between Christ and antichrist during the Great Tribulation. Since Egypt is a type of the world system (as discussed previously), the plagues demonstrate the powerlessness of the false gods of this world.

The Tribulation Plagues

The purpose of the great tribulation is to punish the inhabitants of the earth for their unbelief. During the great tribulation, "a third of the sea became blood; and a third of the living creatures in the sea died" (Rev. 8:8–9, 16:4; cf. Exod. 7:14–25). The Bible teaches that blood has two main purposes: to give physical and spiritual life, or to destroy life. The plague of blood is designed to punish all those who do not believe.

> And I saw three unclean spirits like frogs coming out of the mouth of the dragon, out of the mouth of the beast, and out of the mouth of the false prophet. For they are spirits of demons, performing signs, which go out to the kings of the earth and of the whole world, to gather them to battle of that great day of God Almighty. (Rev. 16:13–14; cf. Exod. 8:1–15).

We notice here that during the Great Tribulation, the plagues move from the natural to the supernatural and from the visible to the invisible. The plague of frogs in Egypt is a prototype of this plague of demons upon the world at the time of the end.

> Then I heard a loud voice from the temple saying to the seven angels, "Go and pour out the bowls of the wrath of God on the earth." So the first went and poured out his bowl upon the earth, and a foul and loathsome sore came upon the men who had the mark of the beast and those who worshipped his image. (Rev. 16:1–2; cf. Exod. 9:9)

109

That painful plague of pestilence afflicts both men and animals. The mystery of animal pain helps us to understand human suffering: "For we know that the whole creation groans and labors with pangs together until now" (Rom. 8:22). Adam's sin brought judgment on man and beast. The whole earth is in a deteriorating condition. This deterioration will continue until the Lord Jesus Christ comes to earth as Prince of Peace.

> The first angel sounded: And hail and fire followed, mingled with blood, and they were thrown to the earth; and a third of the trees were burned up, and all green grass was burned up. (Rev. 8:7; cf. Exod. 9:13–35)

The purpose of this end-time plague is to bring judgment against pantheistic believers who hold that God is in everything. The trees, the grass, and the animals are all part of God according to that belief. ". . . the universe is fundamentally a spiritual reality because everything that exists is God."[12] The New Age movement is leading the world into false worship of creation.

> Then the fourth angel poured out his bowl on the sun, and power was given to him to scorch men with fire. And men were scorched with great heat, and they blasphemed the name of God who has power over these plagues; and they did not repent and give Him glory. Then the fifth angel poured out his bowl on the throne of the beast, and his Kingdom became full of darkness; and they gnawed their tongues because of the pain. And they blasphemed the God of heaven because of their pains and sores, and they did not repent of their deeds" (Rev. 16:8–11; cf. Exod. 10:21–29)

As a thick darkness fell upon all the land of Egypt at the hands of Moses (Exod. 10:22), so likewise "the sun will be darkened, and the moon will not give its light; the stars will fall from heaven, and the powers of the heavens will be shaken" (Matt. 24:29).

As mentioned earlier, the highest deity in Egypt was Ra, meaning "the sun-god". The Egyptians worshipped Ra as the source of light. For this reason, the plague of darkness shows judgment against those who worship the sun. In the same way, the plague of darkness at the end illustrates God's judgment against nature worship.

After total darkness comes on the world, nothing remains except death and final judgment. Moses had been sent by God to deliver the children of Israel from the slave market of Egypt, and because Pharaoh rejected Moses and his God, Pharaoh and his people had to suffer the consequences. God had given Pharaoh and his people enough warnings to repent, but when God's warnings were rejected for the last time, Pharaoh and his people had passed the point of no return. The final judgment upon them was death.

The American media often reports about the seemingly unending slaughter of human beings. Each sunrise reveals thousands of victims around the world, not only those who were killed the day before, but also those who were physically and emotionally injured.

Ironically, war seems to have existed since the beginning of creation. Every generation has witnessed its own war. Parents are becoming reluctant to give birth to children, who may end up victims of war. However, the turmoil in our world has been predicted by the Lord Jesus and by His prophets, but the end of wars and suffering is forthcoming, when the Lord Jesus returns "on the clouds of heaven with power and great glory" (Matt. 24:30). Likewise, the Revelation judgments will result in death for billions of the earth's inhabitants, because they will refuse to repent from their unbelief. The Lord Jesus Christ produces a positive or negative response. A person either becomes softened or hardened, convicted or defiant. One cannot be neutral. When the only Savior of mankind is rejected, there will be the screaming of eternal death, and "There will be wailing and gnashing of teeth" (Matt. 13:50). What a price to pay for being stubborn.

Islam Rejects the Crucifixion

Prior to the birth of Islam, polytheistic worship was practiced in most of the Arab world. Islamic monotheistic belief rejects the doctrines of redemption and the deity of Christ as revealed in the Bible. During my speaking engagements, I meet many Muslims who are searching to find convincing answers to those two biblical doctrines, which Islam emphatically rejects. Here is a summary of what they believe: The Qur'an teaches that a plot was designed to crucify Jesus and an actual execution on the cross took place. Someone was really crucified, but it was not Jesus; it was someone else who was crucified in His place. As for Jesus Himself, God saved Him from a violent death and raised Him up to heaven.

> [The Jews] said: "We killed Christ Jesus the son of Mary, the apostle of God." But they killed him not, nor crucified him, but so it was made to appear to them . . . for of a surety they killed him not. Nay, God raised him up to Himself. (Qur'an 5:153–158; cf. 3:52–59).

Islam rejects the crucifixion of Christ and His vicarious atonement for sins. Islam teaches that no one can make atonement for the sins of another; and since Jesus was neither killed nor crucified, there is no need to believe in the doctrine of redemption. Following are some logical questions Muslims ask to justify such a belief:

> Does the crucifixion of Jesus befit the justice, mercy, and wisdom of God?

> Does God require someone to bear the sins of others on Himself?

> Is it consistent with God's mercy and wisdom to believe that He will allow Jesus to be humiliated and murdered to save others from their sin of unbelief?

> Is it proper to believe that God was unable to forgive Adam and his children for the original sin, and that He held them in suspense until Jesus came to make the atonement with His own blood?

> Does the belief of crucifixion and human sacrifice appear in any religion apart from the pagan creeds of the early Greeks, Romans, Indians, Persians, and the like?

Can a believer imagine that Jesus would speak to God from the cross as He was dying?

Is God that cruel to allow His messenger to suffer at the hands of His enemies?

Islam teaches that Jesus was a great prophet and teacher who fought hypocrisy and blasphemy and was honored by God from the time of His virgin birth until He was taken alive to heaven. That is a synopsis of what the Muslims say when I try to discuss with them the reason Jesus had to die on the cross. In response to their logical deduction and sophistry, I usually share the story of the Passover.

The Passover

The significance and appropriation of the death of Christ on the cross is seen in minute detail in the Passover. The death of Christ and appropriation of His blood, as seen in the Passover, satisfied God's righteous judgement, and His wrath has been averted from believing sinners. The Passover was offered only once in Egypt.

God said to Moses, "This month shall be your beginning of months; it shall be the first month of the year to you" (Exod. 12:1). This was the beginning of a new life with new promises, new hopes, and a new walk. The Hebrews were slaves in Egypt, but they would be rescued from the slave market by blood, and their new birth as a nation would begin as they received the message by faith. Everything that occurred in this story is linked metaphorically to the finished redemptive work of Christ at Calvary, for these things were "written for our learning . . . and they were written for our admonition" (Rom. 15:4; cf. 1 Cor. 10:11).

Abraham and his descendants used the Babylonian method of telling time, so the new year began with the month *Tisri* (October). God wanted the new year to start with the month *Abib* (April), meaning "green sprouts" (Exod. 13:4). Spring brings new life, an illustration of spiritual birth.

113

Israel's new life began fourteen days before the Passover—God wanted the Hebrews to live by faith before seeing the sacrifice of the lamb (Exod. 12:6). Our spiritual new birth does not begin with the sacrifice of our Passover Lamb (Jesus Christ), for He has already been sacrificed once for all. It begins the moment we believe the record that God has given concerning His Son, "having been born again, not of corruptible seed but incorruptible, through the word of God which lives and abides forever" (1 Pet. 1:23). We begin our spiritual new birth by faith before we see any evidence, and we are to continue to live by faith.

> Faith is the substance of things hoped for, the evidence of things not seen. . . . But without faith it is impossible to please Him. (Heb. 11:1–6)

Moses was commanded to speak the following words to the congregation of Israel:

> On the tenth day of this month every man shall take for himself a lamb . . . according to each man's need. (Exod. 12:3–4)

The lamb was to be singled out for death before it was actually killed. The Lord Jesus was marked out for death before He was truly slain.

The Lord Jesus was in Jerusalem between the tenth and the fourteenth of *Nisan* (April), and He became our Passover on the fourteenth day of the month. Josephus tells us that a *paschal* (Passover) company consisted of not less than ten members. The lamb was not only for killing and applying the blood, but also for eating. Every man had to take a lamb for himself and his family and share it with neighbors. Now I understand why our Lord said:

> Most assuredly, I say to you, unless you eat the flesh of the Son of Man and drink His blood, you have no life in you. (John 6:53)

This truth refers to the fact:

Christ died for our sins according to the Scriptures, and that He was buried, and that He rose again the third day according to the Scriptures. (1 Cor. 15:3–4)

God also instructed them concerning the passover that the lamb shall be without blemish, a male of the first year. . . . Now you shall keep it until the fourteenth day of the same month. Thus the whole assembly of the congregation of Israel shall kill it at twilight. (Exod. 12:5–6)

The lamb was to be without any deformity or defect and was to be one year old. A year-old lamb was in the very prime of its life, so it was killed in the fullness of its strength. Christ was "a lamb without blemish and without spot" (1 Pet. 1:19) and was in the prime of His life when He was crucified.

The Lord's Passover began "at twilight" on the fourteenth day of Nisan (Lev. 23:5). The fifteenth of Nisan began a feast lasting for seven days during which unleavened bread was eaten (Lev. 23:6). The first and seventh days were holy sabbath days when no work was allowed (Exod. 12:16).

Christ died on the fourteenth day of Nisan. The next day was a holy day when no work was allowed. Those who took down the body of Christ from the cross were forced to hurry in order to complete their work before the sabbath day came at sundown. That is why they laid Him in a new tomb in a garden near Calvary.

The lamb was to be killed "at twilight, at the going down of the sun" (Deut. 16:6). It was that period of the day, between three and six in the afternoon, when the sun is going down. Mark tells us that it was the third hour (9 A.M.) when they crucified Him (Mark 15:25). At the sixth hour, there was darkness over the whole land of Israel until the ninth hour, "And at the ninth hour Jesus cried out with a loud voice, saying, *"Eloi, Eloi, lama sabachthani?"* (My God, My God why have You forsaken Me?) (Mark 15:34). It was shortly after this that He expired, fulfilling the exact time of the day for the death of the Passover sacrifice. Thus, the sufferings of Christ were written ahead of time in the law of Moses, in the prophets, and in the Psalms (Luke 24:44–46). When I discuss the Passover with inquisitive Muslims, they become more interested in pursuing further dialogue concerning the death of Christ.

Is Jesus God?

It is normal for a Muslim to question the deity of Christ. However, the Lord is blessing the biblical method I use to prove the deity of Christ through the story of the Exodus. Instead of arguing about the Qur'an, I concentrate on the Bible and recount what happened to Egypt during the time of Moses, and I try to show the contrast between the Egyptian gods of the Exodus and the true God. This method will eventually lead to the claim of Christ's deity.

The Egyptians had many gods, and in the ancient world the name of a deity told about that deity. So Moses asked God to tell him about His name, "And God said to Moses, 'I AM WHO I AM' (Exod. 3:14). God's full name is I AM WHO I AM, which has been anglicized as *Jehovah* or *Yahweh*. This name is called the *Tetragrammaton*, because it is composed of only four Hebrew characters. "I AM" is a shorthand form of His name, which is an imperfect tense of the verb *to become*. The tense is indefinite, so it may be translated "I AM," "I WAS," and "I WILL BE." The doubling of the verb, *to be*, signifies eternality and perfection.

When the religious Jews of Jesus' day questioned Him concerning His claim to divinity, Jesus claimed to be the same I AM as Jehovah in the Book of Exodus (John 8:58). To believe in the name of the Lord Jesus Christ is to believe in His person and His work. This is why believing on the name of Christ saves a person (John 1:12, 20:31).

The Septuagint translates Exodus 3:14 as "I am the existing One." John refers this to the Lord Jesus (John 18:6). This name signifies that the Lord Jesus is and was and always will be the same yesterday, today, and forever; the Alpha and the

Omega, the Beginning and the End, who is and who was and who is to come, the Almighty! (Heb. 13:8; Rev. 1:8).

Future Hope for Egypt

In this world, people are influenced by various idolatrous practices, as in the case of ancient Egyptians. Many modern Arabs and Muslims[13] still believe that whatever happens during the course of their lives is caused by spiritual forces who have the power to control human and natural events. (This is a form of spiritism.) The reason God inflicted Egypt with ten plagues was to show His power over the Egyptian gods, and so that His "name may be declared in all the earth" (Exod. 9:16).

In a like manner, Isaiah 19 (like Revelation 9) predicts a future judgment of those who

> did not repent of the works of their hands, that they should not worship demons, and idols of gold, silver, brass, stone, and wood, which can neither see nor hear nor walk; and they did not repent of their murders or their sorceries or their sexual immorality or their thefts. (Rev. 9:20–21)

People cannot predict the future. Even the weather person, who has the scientific knowledge of all sorts of technical devices at his fingertips, is unable to predict the weather for twenty-four hours in advance. Only the person whom the Lord God has chosen to be His prophet can predict accurately. Literal fulfillment of biblical prophecies are among the greatest evidences of the plenary verbal inspiration of the Bible.

Isaiah was one of the prophets whose predictions have been fulfilled with breathtaking accuracy. The theme of Isaiah's book is the Lord and Savior Jesus Christ. The prophet predicted Christ's virgin birth, His life, His holy character, His death, His bodily resurrection, and His Second Coming to this earth to judge the human race and to save a remnant of Arabs, Jews, and Gentiles.

Arabs and Jews will live harmoniously in the days of the glorious reign of Messiah during the millennium. The millennium will be characterized by the binding of Satan for a thousand years (Rev. 20:2) and by a peaceful coexistence of all nations. Then, a perfect sinless state begins after the creation of the new heavens and a new earth (Isa. 65:17, 66:22; 2 Pet. 3:13; Rev. 21:1).

God Restores True Worship

According to John 5:22, God the Father has given all judgment into the hands of God the Son. Rejection of the Savior is the basis of judgment. The result of this is that all unbelievers are cast into the lake of fire (Rev. 20:15). Punishment in hell is eternal separation from God, where the fire is not quenched (Mark 9:44).

The fruits of God's chastisement of unbelievers will usher a new age of unsurpassed peaceful coexistence between Arabs, Jews, and Gentiles. This will be a literal fulfillment of the promise God made to Abraham in Genesis 12:3, "And in you all the families of the earth shall be blessed." In other words, all those entering the millennium will be redeemed by the blood of the Lamb of God (Christ), according to the riches of His grace (Eph. 1:7).

There will be found in Egypt an altar and a memorial pillar dedicated to Yahweh, just as Abraham built an altar to express his gratitude and allegiance to God (Gen. 12:8). Also, Egypt shall express gratitude and allegiance to the Lord and enter into a covenant with Him (Isa. 19:19–21).

The restoration of the Temple on Mount Zion will take place during the millennium. The Temple will be the throne room in which Christ will rule over the nations of the earth. Ezekiel gave a detailed description of the millennial Temple (chapters 40–48). God said to Ezekiel:

118

> son of man, this is the place of My throne and the place of the soles of My feet, where I will dwell in the midst of the children of Israel forever. No more shall the house of Israel defile My holy name. (Ezek. 43:7)

That verse of Scripture teaches that God is angry with those who defile His holy name, but during the millennium the Lord's holy name will be feared and revered by all, and the Egyptians will know the Lord in that day, and will make sacrifice and offerings; yes, they will make a vow to the Lord and perform it (Isa. 19:21).

Since Egypt has been portrayed in this chapter as a type of this world's slave market, and since a remnant of the human race will be redeemed "out of the Great Tribulation, and [wash] their robes and [make] them white in the blood of the Lamb" (Rev. 7:14); then, and only then, will God initiate a lasting peace between Arabs and Jews and all the nations of the earth:

> In that day there will be a highway from Egypt to Assyria, and the Assyrian will come into Egypt and the Egyptian into Assyria, and the Egyptians will serve with the Assyrians. In that day Israel will be one of three with Egypt and Assyria, a blessing in the midst of the land, whom the Lord of hosts shall bless, saying, "Blessed is Egypt My people, and Assyria [Iraq] the work of My hands, and Israel My inheritance." (Isa. 19:23–25)

A highway is used to remove alienation and separation and to open communication between God and His people. Assyria, Egypt, and Israel-represent all the warring nations of the earth. The point being made here is that all the nations of the earth will live in peace under the leadership of the Prince of Peace during the millennium.

MYSTERY, BABYLON THE GREAT

A lthough this book delineates important information about the Semitic peoples of the Middle East, in particular, the reader may have noticed an underlying theme relating to man's redemption through the atoning death of Christ on the cross, which forms a vital theme running through all the chapters of this book.

According to my understanding of Scripture, the inhabitants of the earth are given two choices only: (1) to "seek the Lord [Jesus] while He may be found, call upon Him while He is near" (Isa. 55:6); or (2) to try to reach heaven, as Nimrod tried, and be "judged according to their works" (Rev. 20:12).

There is a balance in the Bible between good and evil, salvation and condemnation. Biblical Arabs and Jews have had good and bad relationships in the past. For instance, Hiram, the king of Tyre and Sidon, helped King David build his palace by sending him cedar wood and skillful workers from Lebanon to Jerusalem (2 Sam. 5:11). He also sent timber to King Solomon and shipped it to Joppa, the port of Jerusalem (1 Kings 5:1). He donated large quantities of gold to Solomon and received twenty towns in Galilee as a gift from Solomon (1 Kings 9:11). Hiram trained Solomon's sailors to sail the Mediterranean (1 Kings 10:22). Arabian tradition maintains that Hiram gave his daughter in marriage to Solomon.

After the death of Hiram, Eth-baal ascended the throne and became the priest of Astarte. His daughter Jezebel became the wife of Ahab, king of Israel (1 Kings 16:31). She was instrumental in establishing idol worship at the court of Ahab. Four hundred and fifty prophets of Baal and four hundred prophets of Astarte were at her disposal (1 Kings 18:19). This evil Lebanese queen not only introduced idolatry to Israel, but she killed the prophets of God and continually harassed Elijah (1 Kings 18:13, 19:2).

Arabs and Jews have had sporadic peaceful accords in recent times. However, they have been appointed to play their roles respectively in God's prophetic plan for the human race.

The reader should be mindful of the signs of the times and remember the command of the Lord Jesus to make disciples of all the nations (Matt. 28:19). Unfortunately, many followers of the Lord Jesus have become preoccupied with prophecy concerning world events, particularly as related by the mass media. Wars in the Middle East have always raised special interest for those Christians enamored with prophecy. Whenever fighting takes place in that part of the world, particularly if Israel is involved, prophecy antennas go up, and the radars are turned on.

The Gulf War of 1991 gave doomsayers a unique opportunity to air their unrestrained predictions concerning a fiery Armageddon and the end of the world. Books on prophecy and the rebuilding of Babylon flooded the market and became bestsellers. Speakers versed in prophecy were interviewed on radio and television programs and were asked to speak to large crowds in churches across North America and abroad.

Many televangelists have been stirring up anger and hate against Iraq and preaching retribution. These men of God seem to carry a vendetta against Saddam Hussein. Many of them identify the Iraqi president as the antichrist. In fact, the harshest and most condemning words have been heard, not from generals and politicians, but from television preachers.

In the past, many teachers of prophecy speculated that the rebuilding of Babylon by Saddam Hussein was a sign of the end times. However, God said:

> Babylon, the glory of Kingdoms, the beauty of the Chaldean's pride, will be as when God overthrew Sodom and Gomorrah. It will never be inhabited, nor will it be settled from generation to generation. (Isa. 13:19-20)

In the past, similar doomsayers postulated that Napoleon, Stalin, Mussolini, Hitler, the King of Spain, the Pope, and other world leaders were the antichrist. Such commercialized prophecy has been continually used to foretell what person will rise to power at the end time. His appearance would herald the last days and the return of the Messiah. It is true that the antichrist and the last days are linked (2 Thess. 2:3–4), but no one knows his true identity but God.

The Rise of Babylonianism

The beginning of the antichristian system of religion is known as Babylonianism. Babylon was a flourishing ancient kingdom that reached its zenith under the leadership of Nebuchadnezzar, king of Babylon (605–560 B.C.). The country and city of Babylon have their roots in the city of Babel (Gen. 11:1–9).

After the Flood, Noah's descendants journeyed to a region in the vicinity of the Garden of Eden and the Euphrates River, part of which may have been the land of Shinar (Gen. 10:10). There, Nimrod, the son of Cush, and his followers founded Babel (Gen. 10:8–10). The word Babel is similar to an Akkadian word meaning "gate of god", since *bab* denotes "door or gate," and *el* is a name for a god. The word *Babel*, is also close in spelling to a Hebrew word that means "confusion". Whatever its meaning, Babel in its zenith, as the city of Babylon, became one of the seven wonders of the world.

The Building of the Tower

Nimrod and his followers built a tower, probably some type of religious edifice. Secular history and archaeological discoveries reveal that a gigantic temple was built in the midst of Babylon for the worship of Belus, later called Baal. Many ancient cities of Mesopotamia (modern Iraq) had these temples. These huge structures, called ziggurats, may have been patterned after the original structure of the biblical Tower of Babel. As James Macqueen has explained:

> In an isolated position immediately opposite the main gate, but towards the west of the courtyard, stood the ziggurat or temple tower of Babylon. This mighty building, rising to a height of almost 300 feet, must have been a dominant feature of the Babylonian landscape, and certainly accounts for the Biblical narrative of the Tower of Babel. Only the ground plan was recovered by excavation, and there has been a great deal of scholarly argument on the details of the upper portion, but thanks to descriptions given by Herodotus and in contemporary inscriptions, the general shape of the building is clear. The tower was square in plan, and rose, probably in eight stages, to a temple at the summit. The lowest stage was 300 feet square and about 108 feet high, the second 256 feet square and 60 feet high. The third, fourth, and fifth stories were each about 20 feet high, with sides of 197 feet, 167 feet and 138 feet. The size and shape of the sixth, seventh and eighth stories are disputed, but it seems most probable that the sixth was 108 feet square and 20 feet high, while the seventh stage, 50 feet high, was no longer square but rectangular, measuring probably 79 feet by 69 feet. On top of this may have been a small "wardroom," the dimensions of which are not known, forming an eighth story. . . . The whole of this structure was apparently faced with baked bricks over a core of unbaked bricks. The core of the first stage was 200 feet square, while the facing on all sides was 50 feet thick, and finished with the usual recesses between flat "towers." The upper stories may also have been finished in this way, but this is not certain.[1]

The Meaning of the Tower

Babel became not only a great city, but also it symbolized a political-governmental system that continues to influence us today. The anti-Christian system of a one-world kingdom (one-world order), as opposed to Christ's theocratic kingdom, can be traced to Nimrod and to the beginning of his kingdom (Gen. 10:10). The construction of the Tower of Babel became a symbol of the spiritual Babylon and of Satan's political and religious system of government throughout the ages.

Babel, or Babylon, was ruled by Nimrod and his beautiful wife Semiramis.[2] Nimrod ruled politically and was the head of the Babylonian state; Semiramis ruled religiously and was the head of the pagan system of religion and idolatry. The tower of Babel and Babylon symbolized politics and religion merged into one great system of world unity that became known as a one-world order. This type of federation was the dream of the Babylonians and has been the dream of mankind ever since.

The word *Nimrod* means "rebel." Nimrod was the first person who had the audacity to establish a kingdom and a system of worship of his own. He organized a world federation on a grand scale and succeeded in forming a religious system centered at the Tower of Babel, where the whole earth had one language and one speech (Gen. 11:1).

Nimrod and his followers wanted to build

a tower whose top is in the heavens [to] make a name for [themselves], lest [they] be scattered abroad over the face of the whole earth. (Gen. 11:4)

Nimrod's plan did not succeed, because the only way to reach heaven and obtain security is through Jesus Christ. The Babylonians and their spiritual descendants have denied God's plan of salvation and eternal security by trying to gain heaven through their own works. The Bible identifies the self-centered spirit of Babylon as the spirit of the antichrist (1 John 2:18–23; 2 John 7). This spiritual attitude is a man-made tower to God, built on a false foundation of salvation by works.

Man's dream has always been to build a super organization that will bring a utopia of peace and happiness. This spirit asserted itself in Egypt under the pharaohs, in Babylon under Nebuchadnezzar, in Greece under Alexander the Great, and in Rome under the caesars. In modern times, Napoleon, Hitler, and others have tried to build utopias. All have failed because man does not learn from history. The German philosopher Hegel said, "We ask men to study history, but the only thing men learn from the study of history is that men learn nothing from the study of history." Hegel's statement seems to be empirically correct as it relates to the facts of history concerning the forming of a new economic and political order. In fact today, a new computer program named Babelfish has the capability of translating documents in other languages into one's own language. Thus, restoring the world to the pre-Babylonian system of speaking one language.

The New World Order

The turmoil in our world has given mankind a reason to look for practical solutions to regulate disputes emanating from economic and political problems. As a result of a deteriorating economic and political disorder, an elite group of Western scholars and politicians has emerged to prevent the world from lapsing into total chaos. This group of people has already established a powerful economic, political, and religious coalition.

Among all the groups that seem to be focusing on a new world order, the Trilateral Commission is by far the most elite of them all. This private organization was founded in 1973 for the purpose of safeguarding the economy and interests of the ruling classes of Western Europe, North America, and Japan. These three allies control more than ninety percent of the world's capital.

The Trilateral Commission has no allegiance to any nation. Its purpose is to secure monetary profits and to control both national and international affairs. The proponents of a one-world system are molding public opinion by publishing and airing documentaries to prepare the way for the new world order.

The Reconstruction of the Tower

There is today a revival of the spirit of Babylonianism, resulting from humanity's pride in its technological and scientific achievements. This pride leaves out God and leads to the belief that people can find peace and prosperity if they will only work together. Satan, as the god of this age, has blinded the minds of such people to the truth, "lest the light of the gospel of the glory of Christ, who is the image of God, should shine on them" (2 Cor. 4:4).

Babylonianism has existed in many different forms, but it has remained basically the same. Babylonianism has two objectives: (1) a political order that denies the right of the Lord Jesus to reign as "KING OF KINGS AND LORD OF LORDS" (Rev. 19:16); and (2) a religious system that denies the authority of Christ and the Scriptures.

Before the coming of the Lord, Satan's kingdom on earth will resemble Nimrod's Babylon. The stage is being set now for the appearance of this corrupt political and religious system. The Bible connects this future man-made system of the apocalypse with ancient Babylon (Rev. 17:5).

In his exhaustive and much-quoted work, *The Two Babylons*, Alexander Hislop draws parallels between apocalyptic Babylon and the Roman Catholic Church, as the following summary of his book reveals:

> The book was written with a wealth of material exposing all idolatrous practices of the Roman Catholic Church, and demonstrating that Rome is Babylon of the Apocalypse. Hislop goes into a great detail to prove that Semiramis was the first woman to be worshipped as the Babylonian goddess of fertility. She also introduced mother and child worship, and such worship did spread throughout the world. The mother became known as "the queen of heaven," who provoked God "to anger" (Jer. 7:18); and whom the Ephesians worshipped as "the great Diana" (Acts 19:23–

35). Her son was known as Tammuz, and his idolization by the Jews provoked God to jealousy. (Ezek. 8:14)[3]

Many authors and theologians came to the same conclusion as Hislop concerning the Roman Catholic Church being the Babylon of the Apocalypse. Although the Roman Catholic Church has inherited many pagan practices from ancient Babylon, the two Babylons of Revelation 17 and 18 represent something larger—a religious global federation. An understanding of these federations begins with Nebuchadnezzer's dream. This vast historical perspective includes Arabs and Jews and the whole of the Middle East.

The Metallic Image

Nebuchadnezzar king of Babylon, had a dream that not one of his wise men could interpret. Daniel finally interpreted the dream by the power of God. The purpose of the dream was to make "known to King Nebuchadnezzar what will be in the latter days" (Dan. 2:28). This means that the scope of the dream records some events within that period of time known as the latter days. Whenever these words are mentioned in the Bible they usually refer to the times of Messianic prophecy (Gen. 49:1; Deut. 4:30, 31:29; Num. 24:14; Jer. 23:20, 30:24, 48:47, 49:39; Ezek. 38:16; Dan. 10:14; Hos. 3:5; Joel 2:28; Mic. 4:1; Acts 2:17–21; 2 Pet. 3:1–4). The interpretation of the latter days seems to include the whole scope of past, present, and future events that are related to the Messiah.

The dream is of a great image of a mighty man with a head of gold, breast and arms of silver, belly and thighs of bronze or copper, legs of iron, and feet of iron and clay mixed (Dan. 2:31–35).

The polymetallic image was terrible to behold. Then, quite suddenly, the great stone appeared in the dream. The stone struck the image upon the feet, and it collapsed and disintegrated into fine particles like powder. And then the wind removed the particles, and the stone which "struck the image became a great mountain and filled the whole earth."

128

Daniel spoke of the Great Stone, the Lord Jesus, who will crush the kingdoms of this world (Dan. 2:34–35, 44). Nations will come and go, but God rules a kingdom that will never be destroyed.

The Golden Head

The four metals represent four successive kingdoms—Babylon, Medo-Persia, Greece, and Rome. The head of gold represented King Nebuchadnezzar and his empire. Daniel said to the king of Babylon, "You are this head of gold" (Dan. 2:38). Jeremiah specified that world dominion was given by God to Nebuchadnezzar at that time:

> I have given all these lands into the hand of Nebucha-dnezzar the King of Babylon, My servant; and the beasts of the field I have given him to serve him. (Jer. 27:5–6)

That is one of the proofs God is able to use unregenerate men and nations to do His will. For instance, God is using the turmoil in the Middle East in particular, to pave the way for the Great Tribulation in which all the nations of the earth will participate (Zech. 14:2).

The Silver Breast and Arms

The breast and two arms of silver symbolized the unification of Medo-Persia. Darius, the Median King, took the kingdom from the last Babylonian king, Belshazzar (Dan. 5:31). Darius and Cyrus, kings of Persia, united to form one kingdom as mentioned in Daniel 8:20. The Medo-Persian kingdom was frequently called the Persian empire.

History does not speak much of a Median empire, neither does the Bible. However, the third son of Japheth is Madai. He was the progenitor of the Medes. The Medes became known as modern Kurds. According to 2 Kings 17:6, after Assyria took Samaria (modern Nablus), around 722 B.C., the king of Assyria deported the Jews to several towns of Media. As a result, the Jews participated in Kurdish life and contributed to it greatly. The Jews in Media (modern Kurdistan) had freedom to share their faith with their Kurdish neighbors, and many of them were converted to Judaism. To this day, Jewish shrines of Daniel's tomb in Hamadan are still in Kurdish towns not far from modern Iraq. Some other prophets may have been buried in Kurdistan, such as Nahum, Jonah, Mordecai, and Habakkuk. In Isaiah 13:17 and Jeremiah 51:11, 28; the Medes are said to have been used by God to destroy Babylon. In Daniel 6:8, it is said that the laws of the Medes "cannot be changed." The Book of Esther sheds much light on the history of the Jews in Media.

The Bronze Belly and Thighs

The belly and thighs of bronze symbolized the Graeco-Macedonian empire, founded by Alexander the Great and continued by his successors. The Bible identifies the third kingdom as Greece (Dan. 8:21).

It has been reported that Alexander was given a copy of the Book of Daniel, in which he was mentioned. The Greek conqueror was so impressed by the prophecy that when he entered the city of Jerusalem, instead of destroying it, he went to the Temple and worshipped God. Daniel predicted that the Greek empire would be divided into four kingdoms (Dan. 8:22). After the death of Alexander, General Cassander ruled Macedonia; General Lysemachus ruled Thrace and Turkey; General Seleucus ruled Syria; and General Ptolemy ruled Egypt (Dan. 8:8).

The Iron Legs and Alloy Feet

The fourth kingdom was Rome, symbolized by the legs of iron with the feet of iron mixed with clay. Although the Bible does not say that Rome succeeded the empire of Greece, secular history records this progression. A logical conclusion is that Rome is the fourth empire envisioned in this prophecy.

The Roman empire was strong as iron (Dan. 2:40). Iron was the strongest and hardest metal in Daniel's time and was used to cut silver, gold, and other weaker metals. Iron is used in this prophecy metaphorically to describe the strength of Rome at its zenith. Rome did conquer all the other kingdoms and destroyed much of their political and national character.

The Roman empire filled the world and was controlled by one person under the title caesar. Rome gave the world an unmatched political and religious unity, as Francis Schaeffer explained:

> Roman civilization is the direct ancestor of the modern western world. From the first conquests of the Roman Republic down to our own day, Roman law and political ideas have had a strong influence on the European scene and the entire western world. Wherever western civilization has gone, it has been marked by the Romans. . . . Augustus was a divinely appointed leader and that Rome's mission was to bring peace and civilization to the world . . . he became the head of the state religion taking the title Pontifex Maximus and urging everyone to worship the spirit of Rome and the genius of the emperor. Later this became obligatory for all the people of the Empire.[4]

In Nebuchadnezzar's dream, the iron of man's kingdom does not mix with clay (Dan. 2:43). This is interpreted to mean that men from the revived Roman system will mingle themselves with the seed of men, without being able to cleave one to another, in the same manner as iron cannot mingle with clay. In other words, iron symbolizes the kingdoms of Rome that cannot produce permanent world unity. This Roman-antichrist system continually attempts to assert itself over men and to mingle with the seed of men, which is the human race. Mingling denotes becoming an accepted part of ordinary human existence. Iron mixed with clay simply means that man can never unite in purpose. Even though, since the time of Nimrod, this has been the constant dream of man. These kingdoms will be destroyed because they are founded upon a human god.

The Deterioration of the Image

The image of Daniel gradually deteriorates. First, deterioration is seen in the worth of metals: gold, silver, bronze, iron, and clay; second, deterioration in position from head to foot; and third, deterioration in power from a great kingdom to an inferior one (Dan. 2:39).

Nebuchadnezzar ruled the world by divine right as an absolute monarch. God gave Nebuchadnezzar total freedom to execute judgment on his earthly kingdom as he pleased, in such a way that

> all peoples, nations, and languages trembled and feared before him. Whomever he wished, he executed; whomever he wished, he kept alive; whomever he wished, he set up; and whomever he wished, he put down. (Dan. 5:19)

The kings of Medo-Persia were not above the law of the land as Nebuchadnezzar was, and they were subject to the laws of their own realm. Alexander the Great and his Greek successors ruled by virtue of their personal gifts, in organizing and controlling their armies. The Roman emperor ruled by the will and choice of the people. The American republic is based on the belief that the government is only by the approval of the governed. Abraham Lincoln said it best: "government of the people, by the people, and for the people."

In Revelation 2–3, authority and moral conduct deteriorate throughout the Church Age, climaxing in the spirit of Laodicea—passion for entertainment and worldly pleasures and neglect for the words of our Lord. There is a slow movement throughout history in the secular and spiritual world, from rule through authority by the spoken word to rule by public opinion, resulting in anarchy and hyperindividualism.

Ten Horns and Ten Toes

The word *Babylon* is a symbol of all false religions that are concocted by man. In agreement with the prophet Daniel and the Apostle John, the Roman system of government will be revived from its deadly wound (Rev. 13:3). This system of government will be comprised of ten nations under the leadership of the antichrist, who will gain mastery over the whole earth for a short time, and will be destroyed by the Lord Jesus at His Second Coming (Rev. 13:1–10).

The revived Roman system of government is symbolized by a beast, who "was different from all the beasts that were before it, and it had ten horns" (Dan. 7:7). These ten horns are ten kings (Dan. 7:24; Rev. 17:12). In the description of the metallic image, ending with the feet, there was no mention of the ten toes (Dan. 2:33). But in the interpretation of the dream, it is further specified that Nebuchadnezzar saw the feet and toes (Dan. 2:41). The toes were a symbol of the kings that were mentioned in verse 44.

The Rise of Antichrist

The beast, or antichrist, is a man who will act in a beastlike manner. He is described as having

> eyes like the eyes of a man, and a mouth speaking pompous words . . . who opposes and exalts himself above all that is called God . . . so that he sits as God in the temple of God, showing himself that he is God. (Dan. 7:8; 2 Thess. 2:4)

The apostle John identified the doctrine of the antichrist:

> You have heard that the Antichrist is coming. . . . Who is a liar but he who denies that Jesus is the Christ? He is antichrist who denies the Father and the Son. (1 John 2:18, 22)

The Final Overthrow of the Image

As the gradual deterioration of character, authority, and moral conduct reaches a point of no return, our Sovereign Lord Jesus shall return to rule the world with a mighty hand.

> And in the days of these kings the God of heaven will set up a kingdom which shall never be destroyed; and the kingdom shall not be left to other people; it shall break in

pieces and consume all these kingdoms, and it shall stand forever. Inasmuch as you saw that the stone was cut out of the mountain without hands, and that it broke in pieces the iron, the bronze, the clay, the silver, and the gold, the great God has made known to the king what will come to pass after this. The dream is certain, and the interpretation is sure. (Dan. 2:44-45)

The overthrow of all these kingdoms will include the overthrow of "MYSTERY, BABYLON THE GREAT, THE MOTHER OF HARLOTS AND OF THE ABOMINATIONS OF THE EARTH" (Rev. 17:5).

This will end man's worship of himself and his achievements, which is idolatry, the true spirit of Babylonianism.

Deliverance From Idols

The spirit of Babylonianism has been with us from the earliest times. The religion of the past will certainly be the majority religion of the future. The New Age teachings that abound on every hand are preparing the public to receive Babylonian idolatry with its whole heart. There is much discussion today of a new world order. It is necessary at this juncture, for the benefit of the reader, to review the insights of our Reformation forebears concerning the evil of Babylonian idolatry.

The New Testament teaches that idolatry is the worship of a deity other than the Lord Jesus. This is called spiritual idolatry. Physical idolatry occurs when images or other material objects are worshipped as a deity. God hates such idolatrous worship.

The Old Testament is replete with instances where the Hebrews imitated their heathen neighbors in worshiping idols. Idolatry was regarded in the Mosaic codes as a great offense against God. As a result of disobedience, God used Assyria as the rod of [His] anger to punish the Hebrews for worshipping idols and performing wicked deeds (Isa. 10:5–11).

Similarly, God used Islam to destroy much of Christianity's corrupted form of worship during the Dark Ages. Moreover, He is still using Islam to intimidate the lukewarm church of Christ (Rev. 3:16). Christians may pray for a great revival, but how can a sick Bride of Christ be revived by lukewarm preaching and moral decay?

Spiritual and physical idolatry are an evil to be shunned. However, worship of the spirits behind the idols is an even greater evil. There was a time, perhaps like the present, when the church was held in the grip of a false gospel propagated by false gods. God in His mercy sent strong men, Wycliffe, Huss, and Luther to recover the gospel in its simplicity and to put to death the false gods, who were threatening to overwhelm the flock of Christ. Perhaps we can discern more of the Babylonian error of our day and the simplicity of the gospel by looking briefly at the teachings of these men.

John Wycliffe, born in 1329, wrote, in about 1380, against the idolatrous abuses by the established church powers. He sometimes has been called the proto-reformer or the morningstar of the Reformation because of his early anticipation of the works of Luther and Calvin. Wycliffe's various positions can be briefly summarized:

> He accepted the Bible as the one sure basis of belief and demanded that it should freely be placed in lay hands. . . . He restricted the true Church to those persons whom God had predestined to salvation. He rejected the doctrine of transubstantiation as a historical novelty and as philosophically unsound. . . . Upon the Papal Supremacy Wycliffe had long cast doubts: he had likewise advocated clerical marriage, denounced monasticism and placed fanatical emphasis upon the need to disendow a rich and mundane clergy.[5]

In those things he greatly influenced John Huss, the great Bohemian preacher and martyr, and then Huss, in turn, would anticipate the works of Martin Luther, John Calvin, and the rest of the reformers. The preaching of the reformers grew out of the questions that confront all people. The prophet Job stated it well:

135

how can a man be righteous before God? If one wished to contend with Him, he could not answer Him one time out of a thousand. God is wise in heart and mighty in strength. Who has hardened himself against Him and prospered? (Job 9:2–4)

That is the great question, and that is the great God with whom we have to deal. The answer to the question, How can a man be right with God? is more important than silver and gold. It is more important than ecclesiastical power and politics.

We are compelled, as human beings, to continue to meditate upon that question. God has made us like that, for "He has put eternity in [our] hearts" (Eccles. 3:11).

Wycliffe, Huss, and others were raised up by God to bring man's compelling question into the light of day and to discuss the truth and error of the church's position.

Idolatry is the worship or adoration of any visible or invisible thing that is not the true God (cf. John 17:3). The apostle Paul identified serving the true God as turning away from idols.

The Apostle John said that

Jesus Christ . . . is the true God and [we should] keep [ourselves] from idols. (1 John 5:20–21)

The worship of the true God is identical with the worship of the Lord Jesus Christ. Any system of teaching that diverts us from true worship is an idolatrous system.

Obviously, we stand in great need of a new generation of idol breakers—men who can correctly teach us who is the true God and lead us into worship.

The reformers were confronted with a system of teaching that led worship away from the true God. Exactly what were some of the abuses that they confronted? The sale of indulgences was the spark that ignited a fire in the life of Huss as well as in Luther.

John Huss (1372–1415) wrote major treatises against the sale of indulgences, primarily concerning a papal decree from

Pope John XXIII (not of Vatican II fame). An indulgence is a decree from a papal ambassador that all sins of the penitent are remitted. However, the price for this indulgence was to take up arms against King Ladislas of Naples, who had taken the city of Rome and had dislodged Pope John:

> The pope promised "to all truly penitent and confessed," who would take up the cross (i.e., arms) either at their own expense or who would equip and support a soldier for a month, "remission of such of their sins of which they were heartily contrite and which they had confessed."[6]

Huss protested this moneymaking scheme in support of a war effort by the church. He was also led into a critique of the decree under various headings. The first topic with which Huss dealt was the remission of sins. He stated the obvious Scriptural conclusion that the remission of sins was God's prerogative alone. The minister can declare God's forgiveness generally on the basis of true repentance and faith in the Son, but this warrant comes from Scripture not from any person's authority alone. Forgiveness comes from the grace of God alone.

The second topic was material gain, which was the main point behind the sale of these indulgences. This money was to be used by Pope John in a Crusade against the king of Naples. Huss declared that the clergy should agree with Christ's words:

> My kingdom is not of this world. If My kingdom were of this world, My servants would fight, so that I should not be delivered to the Jews; but now My kingdom is not from here. (John 18:36)

In like manner, modern evangelicals have inherited the ecclesiastical spirit of mendacity as evidenced by constant appeals for money in order to promote their ministries.

The third topic concerned the blasphemous nature of the whole proposal. In granting remission of sins in the Pope's name, or the seller's name, it presupposed the ability of a sinful man to grant the Holy Spirit to another man. Furthermore, if man has this ability, why restrict it to a few people; instead, why not save the whole population of the world?[7]

Besides Huss's devastating critiques, we should add that the practice of indulgence-selling deifies man; that is, some men assume godlike powers in order to justify other men before God. This leads away from adoration of the Lord Jesus Christ and toward subservience and adoration of other men, which is idolatry.

Martin Luther (1483–1546) made further connections between the sale of indulgences and the entire system of medieval Christianity. In *The Babylonian Captivity of the Church* Luther railed against his adversaries, Dr. Eck and Jerome Emser:

> Indulgences are evils devised by the toadies at Rome. Meantime Eck, Emser, and their compeers began to read me a lesson on the primacy of the pope. Lest I should appear to be ungrateful to such learned men, I hereby confess that their works have benefitted me greatly. Although I denied divine jurisdiction to the papacy, I admitted a human jurisdiction. But when I had heard and read the most ingenious argument put forward by these five gentlemen to establish their idol in a workmanlike manner, and as I am not entirely lacking in intelligence in such matters, I saw clearly that the papacy was to be understood as the kingdom of Babylon and the regime of Nimrod, the mighty hunter.[8]

Alexander Hislop in *The Two Babylons* published in 1853, reviewed the history and development of the Babylonian system of worship. Luther was also aware of this history and saw Babylonian infiltrations into Christ's flock that needed to be exposed.

As Hislop showed, the names of Nimrod and Semiramis change many times throughout pagan history as their devotees worship a powerful ruler-god and his female consort. From time to time the story changes, and worship is directed toward Semiramis and her child-son, who is also Nimrod.

Many examples can be found of this old pagan story, such as Isis and Osiris in Egypt, Isi and Iswara in India, Fortuna and Jupiter the boy in Rome, and Irene and Plutus in Greece.[9]

In Assyria, this pair were worshipped under the names of Rhea and Tammuz and had infiltrated into the common worship of the Hebrew people. Ezekiel is astounded at the Lord's revelation to him:

> So He brought me to the door of the north gate of the Lord's house; and to my dismay, women were sitting there weeping for Tammuz. (Ezek. 8:14)

This Tammuz was a pagan deity who died and rose again. This event the ancients celebrated with a forty-day period of alternate weeping and rejoicing.[10]

The prophet Jeremiah was rebuked by the people of his day who thought that this Rhea, or Semiramis, was the provider of their abundance. They had forgotten the true God. The Hebrews said to Jeremiah:

> As for the word that you have spoken to us in the name of the Lord, we will not listen to you! But we will certainly do whatever has gone out of our own mouth, to burn incense to the queen of heaven and pour out drink offerings to her, as we have done, we and our fathers, our kings and our princes, in the cities of Judah and in the streets of Jerusalem. For then we had plenty of food, were well-off, and saw no trouble. But since we stopped burning incense to the queen of heaven and pouring out drink offerings to her, we have lacked everything and have been consumed by the sword and by famine. The women also said, "And when we burned incense to the queen of heaven and poured out drink offerings to her, did we make cakes for her, to worship her, and pour out drink offerings to her without our husband's permission?" Then Jeremiah spoke . . . "The Lord could no longer bear it, because of the evil of your doings and because of the abominations which you committed. Therefore your land is a desolation, an astonishment, a curse, and without an inhabitant, as it is this day." (Jer. 44:16–22)

Huss and Luther saw corrupt practices in their day. Luther attacked first the practice of selling indulgences, then the whole sacramental system as a means of salvation. The Babylonian religious system is ever with us; whether in false teaching in the church, or in obviously pagan practices, such as astrology, mind control, and the New Age movement. In breaking the bondage of Babylonian idolatry, Luther cleared the path for righteousness and freedom. In a short treatise entitled *Freedom of a Christian*, Luther expounded the freedom unto which we are called:

> One thing, and only one thing, is necessary for Christian life, righteousness, and freedom. That one thing is the most holy Word of God, the gospel of Christ, as Christ says, John 11:25, "I am the resurrection and the life; he who believes in me, though he die, yet shall he live." . . . On the other hand, there is no more terrible disaster with which the wrath of God can afflict men than a famine of the hearing of his Word, as he says in Amos 8:11. Likewise there is no greater mercy than when he sends forth his Word, as we read in Psalm 107:20. . . . You may ask, "What then is the Word of God, and how shall it be used. . . . The Word is the gospel of God concerning his Son, who was made flesh, suffered, rose from the dead, and was glorified through the Spirit who sanctifies.[11]

God has given many warnings to those who are practicing physical and spiritual idolatry; he said,

> [They] allow that woman Jezebel [Babylonian system of worship and conduct], who calls herself a prophetess, to teach and beguile My servants to commit sexual immorality and to eat   things sacrificed to idols. And I gave her time to repent of her sexual immorality, and she did not repent. Indeed I will cast her into a sickbed, and those who commit adultery with her into great tribulation, unless they repent of their deeds. And I will kill her children with death. And all the churches shall know that I am He who searches the minds and hearts. And I will give to each one of [them] according to your works. (Rev. 2:20–23)

The key word in this passage is *repentance*. The biblical doctrine of repentance has been diluted by those who wanted to exclude it from the gospel message of Christ. "The doctrine of repentance is the missing note in many otherwise orthodox and fundamentally sound circles today."[12] The Lord Jesus Himself warned, "Unless you repent you will all likewise perish" (Luke 13:3, 5).

We must recognize the dangers of "easy-believism" through shallow preaching and teaching about man's total depravity and guilt. Bible colleges and seminaries are producing today many lukewarm preachers and professors who do not give evidence of regeneration.

The Greek word for repentance is *metanoia*; the prefix *meta* means "after" and *noio*, "to understand." *Metanoia* literally means "change of mind and purpose." Biblically it means turning from the sin of unbelief and from the old lifestyle, and turning to God for salvation. In other words, repentance is comprised mainly of two elements: (1) turning to God for salvation, and (2) turning from a lifestyle of sin.

There can be no genuine repentance without these two elements. Therefore, salvation is given only to those who have

> turned to God from idols to serve the living and true God, and to wait for His Son from heaven, whom He raised from the dead, even Jesus who delivers us from the wrath to come! (1 Thess. 1:9–10)[13]

Seven

THE GARDEN OF GOD

T he purpose of this chapter is to establish the geographical location of the River Eden and its tributaries and to
present a brief hypothesis concerning the Garden of Eden,
which was used by God as a symbol of Christ's theocratic
kingdom on earth, instituting the doctrine of salvation by faith
for the benefit of the whole human race.

The traditional site of the Garden of Eden has received
little systematic research in modern times. The rare courses
in this field are limited to a few graduate schools and offered
as subsidiary to archaeological studies. Nowhere are such
courses given as a key to further investigation of pre-Arabic
biblical history. It was not until the 1991 Gulf War that the
American public became informed about the biblical importance of Iraq, the cradle of civilization.

The exact location of the Garden of Eden has completely
baffled Bible scholars and reliable historians. These scholars have rigorously searched for the first residence of man,
and they have left no locality on earth that is similar to the
description of the first abode of mankind unexamined. The
area of the river that went out of Eden to water the garden
remains to this day a bewilderment to adventurous theorists.

The text of Genesis 2:8–14 gives the geographical position
of the Garden of Eden:

> The Lord God planted a garden eastward in Eden, and
> there He put the man whom He had formed. . . . Now a

river went out of Eden to water the garden, and from there it parted and became four riverheads. The name of the first is Pishon; it is the one which encompasses the whole land of Havilah, where there is gold. And the gold of that land is good. Bdellium and the onyx stone are there. The name of the second river is Gihon; it is the one which encompasses the whole land of Cush. The name of the third river is Hiddekel; it is the one which goes toward the east of Assyria. The fourth river is Euphrates.

God planted the garden in the eastern portion of the region of Eden. The river that went forth through Eden watered the garden and was divided into four distinct streams, two of which have been clearly identified as the Tigris (Hiddekel), and the Euphrates (Frat). Their identification has never been disputed, except by those who assume that the whole narrative of Genesis 2:8–14 is a myth or an allegory.

Allegorical Interpretation of Eden

Philo thought that Eden, meaning "pleasure", was a symbol of the soul that delights in enjoyment and exults in virtue. He said, "Now virtue is tropically called paradise, and the site of paradise is Eden, that is, pleasure."[1] The four rivers, according to Philo, are the several virtues of prudence, temperance, courage, and justice.

Many Christian fathers and others agreed with Philo on an allegorical interpretation of Eden. Origen, according to Luther, conceived of paradise as heaven, and the trees as angels. Clement of Alexandria, Papias, Irenaeus, and Pantanus all favored the mystical interpretation of Eden.

Literal View of Eden

Among the Hebrew traditions enumerated by Jerome, paradise (Eden) was created before the world was formed. Some contend that paradise was on a mountain, and they place it between the earth and the firmament; while others have thought that paradise was formerly created on earth but had been destroyed by the judgment of God. Morinus believed that the whole earth was paradise before the Fall and was actually situated in Eden, where there were all kinds of pleasures. Morinus seems to suggest that Eden is a specific place within the whole of the earth where God chose to create man and civilization. There is no end to speculations like these concerning the dimensions of the garden and the locality of Eden; however, two physical locations can be suggested for Eden.

One location for the Garden of Eden may be where the Tigris and Euphrates presently meet. The Pishon and Gihon were thought to be certain portions of the Tigris and Euphrates. Another location may be in Armenia, with the Tigris and Euphrates being placed there. Theologians and historians have supported both views.

The river that went forth from Eden to water the garden continues to be an enigma. Josephus[2] and John of Damascus[3] contend that the four rivers flowed from the ocean stream that surrounded the earth. Those who place the Garden of Eden where the Tigris and Euphrates meet, believe that Shatt-al-Arab was the source from which the four riverheads flowed. Shatt-al-Arab now flows through a broad delta that contains the world's largest date-palm groves and supplies fresh water to south Iraq and Kuwait. This suggested location presents beautiful biblical types of eternal life (fresh water) and physical sustenance (the date-palm).

Those who refer the Garden of Eden to the land of Armenia hold that the river from which the four streams flow is a collection of springs. Only one of the four rivers, the Euphrates, is mentioned by name. The other three are defined by their geographical location.

The River Pishon

Josephus[4] agreed with Eusebius, Epiphanus, Jerome, and Augustine that the Pishon is the Ganges River flowing southeast from the Himalayas in North India. Others believe that the Pishon is the Nile, or the Indus in South Asia, flowing from West Tibet through Kashmir and Pakistan and spilling over into the Arabian Sea.

Some scholars maintained that the Pishon took its rise near Damascus and identified it with the modern Barada River. Others mentioned that the Pishon is the Gozan of 2 Kings 17:6, and from the results of extensive observations in Armenia were "led to infer that the rivers known by the comparatively modern names of Halys and Araxes are those which, in the book of Genesis, have the names of Pishon and Gihon; and that the country within the former is the land of Havilah . . . is the still more remarkable country of Cush."[5]

The majority of those trying to identify Pishon search for it before looking for the location of Havilah. They also use the same method to trace the positioning of the remaining riverheads.

Genesis 2:11–12 describes Havilah as the land that is surrounded by the Pishon River and a place where the best gold and other precious stones are found. The exact location of the Pishon River, "which encompasses the whole land of Havilah," might be identified with the Arabian Gulf (Persian Gulf); and the land of Havilah might have included the modern countries of Yemen, Oman, and Bahrain. Archaeologists have discovered recently Sumerian cuneiform inscriptions identifying the modern country of Oman with ancient Makan. This area of the Persian Gulf flourished in industry and the mining of precious metals and the production of aromatic spices. More than 3000 years ago, ancient Oman flourished in copper ore and also was and still is the source of frankincense. Miners from Makan dug and processed tons of copper ore and exported it through Dilmun, modern Bahrain, to Sumer.[6] Sumerian tablets, discovered in modern Iraq, clearly confirm this information.

Gold, the most valuable of metals, was used as an emblem of nobility and purity (Job 23:10). Gold was known from the very earliest times, and it was at first used primarily for ornamentation (Gen. 24:22). The main producers of gold in biblical times were Sheba, Ophir, and Arabia. Sheba and

Ophir are two of the thirteen Arabian sons of Joktan (a descendant of Noah through Shem), living in the Arabian Peninsula. In Job 22:24, the word Ophir is used for gold. Sheba was another important son of Joktan:

> His tribe colonized southern Arabia and became known as the kingdom of Sheba. . . . This kingdom embraced a vast part of Yemen and was greatly blessed with gold, frankincense, and myrrh. These same gifts were given to the Christ, and they are held to be the kinds of gifts Abraham had given to his six sons through Keturah. (Gen. 25:6)[7]

Psalm 72:15 speaks of the gold of ancient Yemen being given to Christ, the Messiah: "And the gold of Sheba will be given to Him." The land of Havilah was colonized by Havilah and his descendants. Havilah was one of the thirteen sons of Joktan (Gen. 10:29). "It is commonly thought that the district of Khawlan in Yemen was the location of Havilah."[8] Khawlan lies in the northwestern section of Yemen, embracing a large, fertile territory with an unusual abundance of water.

Joktan, the son of Eber (a great-grandson of Noah through Shem) was the father of the thirteen Arabian sons (Gen. 10:25–29). It is assumed that the Joktanites intermarried with Ishmael's descendants and occupied a large portion of the Yemen, dwelling from Havilah as far as Shur, which is east of Egypt in the direction of Assyria (Gen. 25:18). The descendants of Joktan and Ishmael may have settled in Havilah, since Arabs did colonize this area.

William Smith seems to agree with this opinion about the early settlement of Arabs. He asserts that the same country

> is mentioned as forming one of the boundaries of Ishmael's descendants (Gen. xxv. 18), and the scene of Saul's war of extermination against the Amalekites (I Sam. xv. 7). In these passages Havilah seems to denote the desert region southeast of Palestine. But the word occurs also as the proper name of a son of Joktan, in close juxtaposition with Sheba and Ophir, also sons of Joktan and descendants of

Shem (Gen. x. 29), who gave their names to the spice and gold countries of the south. . . . If, therefore, the Havilah of Gen. ii. be identical with any one of these countries, we must look for it on the east or south of Arabia, and probably not far from the Persian Gulf. In other respects, too, this region answers to the conditions required.[9]

The River Gihon

After having established the location of the first river and the land of Havilah as pre-Arabic in population, we need to look for the second river:

The name of the second river is Gihon; it is the one which encompasses the whole land of Cush. (Gen. 2:13)

Cush was the eldest son of Ham (Gen. 10:6). The descendants of Cush may have settled in Ethiopia, that section of Africa close to Egypt and the Red Sea. Some believe Cush was the progenitor of the black race and the founder of Ethiopia. Ethiopia was known to the Greeks as Africa. Others, however, say "the Cushites intermixed with other races and may have been Semitized after they arrived in the Sudan."[10]

The Gihon River has been identified as the Indus River, the Araxes of Armenia, and numerous other rivers in Europe and Asia, but none of these identifications satisfies the required conditions.

Making the Gihon River of paradise the Nile seems more plausible. The reason for this is that the Gihon River is the one which encompasses the whole land of Cush (Gen. 2:13). There is every reason to believe that the land of Cush is Africa and it was occupied by the descendants of Cush, the eldest son of Ham (Gen. 10:6). It would seem that Cush was named from the older country of Genesis 2:13, because many ancient countries connected their lands with paradise, or with the earliest ages of mankind. Cush is identified with Africa, however descendants of Cush spread up to Babylon, as indicated by the city-building activity of Nimrod who is a son of Cush (Gen. 10:8–10).

In the ancient Egyptian inscriptions Ethiopia . . . is termed Keesh or Kesh, and this territory probably perfectly corresponds to the African Cush of the Bible. The Cushites however had clearly a wider extension. . . . The settlement of the sons and descendants of Cush mentioned in Gen. x. may be traced . . . to Babylon, and probably on to Nineveh . . . and Nimrod reigned in Babylonia, and seems to have extended his rule over Assyria. Thus the Cushites appear to have spread along tracts extending from the higher Nile to the Euphrates and Tigris.[11]

The Nile River is mentioned in Jeremiah 2:18 as an equivalent with the word *Sihor* or *Shihor*, meaning "black" or "turbid stream" (cf. Josh. 13:3; Isa. 23:3). Sihor or Shihor is used to describe the different degrees of dark colors, or faces tanned by the sun, or extreme blackness. Jerome in his translation of this passage in Jeremiah, identified Sihor in Egypt as Gihon, and stated:

I myself have seen the waters of Gihon, have seen them with my bodily eyes. It is this Gihon to which Jeremiah points when he says, "What hast thou to do in the way of Egypt to drink the muddy water of Gihon?"[12]

The Nile River has witnessed many events of sacred history. Apart from being the artery of Egypt and other parts of Africa, the Nile is constantly before us in biblical history. Into it the baby Moses was laid in a papyrus boat to save his life (Exod. 2:3). It provided sustenance for Abraham and Jacob and their respective families during the great famines (Gen. 12:10, 46:3–50:26). Tradition tells us that when Joseph and Mary brought our Lord Jesus into Egypt to protect Him from Herod (Matt. 2:13–21), they may have travelled to Heliopolis (the city of the sun), which was by the side of the Nile.

The Nile is the longest river in the world. It flows through parts of Egypt, Sudan, Ethiopa, Kenya, Uganda, Rwanda, Burundi, and Zaire. In the second century A.D., the geographer Ptolemy maintained that the Nile had its source in the heart of Africa at the equator. In 1888, Henry Stanley's research proved Ptolemy's discovery to be substantially correct. The Nile starts below the equator, near Burundi and Zaire and travels more than 4000 miles (about 7000 kilometers) to reach Cairo, then spills over into the Mediterranean Sea.

The Nile is mentioned with the Euphrates in the promise God made to Abraham:

> To your descendants I have given this land, from the river of Egypt to the great river, the River Euphrates. (Gen. 15:18)

This promise seems to support the belief that the Gihon River is the same as the Nile. Moreover, Bible prophecies connect the Euphrates with the Nile, when God will cause them to dry up in the last day (Isa. 19:5; Ezek. 30:12; Zech. 10:10–11; Rev. 9:14, 16:12).

The River Hiddekel

The geographical location of the Tigris and the Euphrates remains to be identified, but the Tigris probably is the third river:

> Now the name of the third river is Hiddekel; it is the one which goes toward the east of Assyria. (Gen. 2:14)

The name of the third river in the Hebrew is *Hiddekel*, meaning "swift, sharp." The Hiddekel is the ancient name of the Tigris. The Babylonians used to call it *Idigla* or *Diglat*. Modern Arabs still call it *al-Dijlah* or *al-Diglah*. In Greek it is called *Tigris*. The name now in use among the inhabitants of Iraq is *Dijleh*. Some writers tell us that the river received its name from its rapidity. The word *Tigris* in the Medo-Persian language is *Tigra*, meaning "an arrow." The name of the Tigris river of Eden in the inscriptions of Assyria is *Tiggar*.

The Tigris rises from a mountain range in East Turkey called the Taurus, flows through Iraq to meet the Euphrates (which then forms the Shatt-al-Arab) and spills into the Persian Gulf. Ancient cities of Mesopotamia that stood on the banks of the Tigris included Seleucia, Nineveh, and the ancient Assyrian city of Asshur. "In ancient times the Tigris entered separately into the Persian Gulf; now it joins the Euphrates and mingles with its waters for more than one hundred miles in the Shatt-al-Arab before entering the Persian Gulf."[13]

After the Flood (Gen. 6–8), the Tigris, along with the other rivers of Eden, may have shifted into different geographical dimensions forming many tributaries. It is interesting to note that modern Iraq is approximately coextensive with ancient Mesopotamia and its life still centers on the two flowing rivers: the Tigris and the Euphrates.

The Tigris "appears indeed under the name of Hiddekel, among the rivers of Eden (Gen. 2:14) and is there described as running eastward to Assyria."[14] Assyria derives its name apparently from Asshur, the second son of Shem (Gen. 10:22). The capital of Assyria was Nineveh (Gen. 10:11). Assyria was a small country in the earliest times but gradually became a great and powerful empire, comprising the whole region bounded by the Armenian mountains in the north, Iraq in the south, the mountains of Kurdistan in the east, and the Mesopotamian desert in the west. In the west it reached to the Euphrates.

Many historians have reported that the richest region of all was the whole country between the Euphrates and the Tigris extending from Assyria even into Arabia (Arabian Peninsula) and Syria. Nineveh was the nucleus of Assyria, and its library of cuneiform tablets, discovered by archaeologists, proved invaluable in understanding the history of this early period of the environs of Eden.

The story of Assyria and its capital on the Tigris, Nineveh, is woven into biblical narrative by the prophets. Nahum and Zephaniah delivered prophecies of Assyria's complete destruction (Nah. 2:8–13; Zeph. 2:13–15). However, before the fulfillment of these prophecies took place, God sent Jonah to preach a revival in Nineveh. Nineveh was built by Nimrod the son of Cush (Gen. 10:8, 11), and Jonah's preaching occurred at a time when Assyria's cruelty had become legendary. The story of Jonah emphasizes God's loving concern for all mankind. Jonah preached, and the greatest revival of all time took place.

> The entire city of Nineveh repented and believed God, proclaimed a fast, and put on sackcloth, from the greatest to the least of them. . . . Then God saw their works, that they turned from their evil way; and God relented from the disaster that He had said He would bring upon them, and He did not do it. (Jon. 3:5–10)

The River Euphrates

"The fourth river is the Euphrates" (Gen. 2:14). The Euphrates, meaning "the good and abounding river," is the only one that was mentioned by its current name from among the four rivers of Eden (Gen. 2:14). The Euphrates, called by the Arabs *al-Furat*, is the longest and the most important river of western Asia. It has furnished a line of traffic between the East and the West, and merchants have used it constantly on their way from the Mediterranean Sea to Babylon. It has been said that Alexander the Great brought ships that had been built in Phoenicia and Cyprus to Babylon by the Euphrates route.

The source of the Euphrates rises from the Armenian mountains and flows through east central Turkey, Syria, and Iraq; and after mingling with the Tigris River and other tributaries to form the Shatt-al-Arab, the waters empty into the Persian Gulf. The Euphrates is mentioned numerous times in Scripture, as in the covenant God made with Abraham, where the whole country of Canaan was promised to Abraham's descendants (Gen. 15:18); more details are found in Deuteronomy and Joshua at the time of the settlement in Canaan (Deut. 1:7, 11:24; Josh. 1:4).

King David was the first to fully enjoy the Promised Land by virtue of his conquests, and Solomon inherited his father's dominions and "reigned over all kingdoms from the River

(Euphrates) to . . . the border of Egypt" (1 Kings 4:21). The original promise of Genesis 15:18 seems to have been ful-filled during the time of Solomon, when his dominion in-cluded almost the whole land of Canaan from the Euphrates in the northeast to the river of Egypt (Nile) in the southwest.

Location of Eden

The location and identity of the four rivers of paradise can be discussed with some clarity, but the location of Eden remains a mystery to historians and Bible scholars.

The description of Eden is as follows:

> The Lord God planted a garden eastward in Eden. . . . Now a river went out of Eden to water the garden, and from there it parted and became four riverheads. (Gen. 2:8–10)

The Scripture says that the garden was planted in the east-ern portion of the region of Eden. If my identity of the four streams is correct, then the location of Eden must have been in ancient Mesopotamia near modern Baghdad. "The lower region of the Tigris-Euphrates valley was the traditional site of the garden of Eden."[15] Mesopotamia is now modern Iraq. The term *Mesopotamia* refers to the upper region of the Tigris-Euphrates valley and embraces also the lower part of the val-ley. The valley is known today by the Arabs as *al-Jazira* (the island). Iraq is the cradle of civilization and probably the site of the first home of man. A number of civilizations have flour-ished in that part of the world, including the Sumerians, the Akkadians, the Babylonians, and the Assyrians. Iraq is approxi-mately coextensive with ancient Mesopotamia. Iraq is bordered by Kuwait, the Arabian Gulf (Persian Gulf), and Saudi Arabia on the south; by Jordan and Syria on the west; by Turkey on the north; and by Iran on the east.

Iraq is an authentic treasure-house of antiquities, and re-cent archaeological excavations have given evidence of its bib-lical importance. It is of utmost significance to remember that the book of Genesis "locates the beginning of human life in the very region which scientific archaeology has demonstrated to be the cradle of civilization."[16] Albright concurs with this opinion by saying:

> no focus of civilization in the earth . . . can begin to compete in antiquity and activity with the basin of the eastern Mediterranean and the region immediately to the east of it.[17]

Typological Interpretation of Eden

The Old Testament is replete with typology and symbolism. The Garden of Eden may be a type of Christ's theocratic kingdom on this earth. God foreknew that the first Adam would rebel against Him and that the whole earth would come under the curse of sin (Gen. 3:17). God predetermined in eternity past to provide the free gift of His glorious salvation to demonstrate "His own love toward us, in that while we were still sinners, Christ died for us. . . . We shall be saved from wrath through Him" (Rom. 5:8–9).

If our location of Eden is correct, God chose a special place near modern Iraq to symbolize His spiritual kingdom. First of all, the reason for planting a garden eastward in Eden is because God wanted to emphasize the fact that the Lord Jesus was born in the east and will return in His glory into the temple by way of the gate which faces toward the east (Ezek. 43:4). Even the wise men saw "His star in the east and [came] to worship Him" (Matt. 2:2).

The good news of Christ's gospel started in the Middle East and permeated the world. Also, the river which became four riverheads, and the tree of life were located in the Middle East.

The tree of life represents the Lord Jesus, because He is the giver of eternal life.[18] The river is a type of the Holy Spirit who gives believers rivers of living water" (John 4:10).

The Garden of Eden is called the "garden of God" (Ezek. 28:13, 31:8–9). The reason for this is that God planted it Himself in order to introduce His glorious salvation plan, which is the most important theme in the entire Bible, and also to introduce the doctrine of free will. The garden was completely furnished with all kinds of vegetation, but God gave special attention to the tree of life and the tree of knowledge.

The tree of life represents the Lord and Savior Jesus Christ, who is the author of eternal life. The tree of knowledge of good and evil was planted in the garden for the purpose of allowing man to exercise his free will to choose between obeying or disobeying the commandments of God, whereby he would be acquitted or judged according to his works (Rev. 20:13).

The tree of knowledge of good and evil represents testing the faith of those who claim a belief in God. Man has been exposed to temptation and trials from the very beginning of history. Abraham was commanded to sacrifice Isaac on Mount Moriah. Abraham obeyed and was rewarded for passing the test. Others have failed the test of faith and were punished for their evil deeds.

Perhaps the tree of knowledge of good and evil was a fig tree. This conjecture is based upon the fact that Adam and Eve did eat from the forbidden fruit of the tree, and when their eyes were opened they sewed fig leaves together and made themselves coverings (Gen. 3:7). Thereafter, God cursed the serpent (Satan) and promised a future victory for the human race. This potentially includes all the descendants of Adam and Eve. This promise of the coming Seed is called the protevangelium (the first mention of the gospel), meaning that man will ultimately triumph over sin and death through the coming Savior (Gen. 3:15).

The sun rises from the east and gives light and physical life to the earth. The sun is a type of Christ, who is the giver of all life, both temporal and eternal; and He is the light of the world (John 8:12). In Psalm 19:1–6, the sun is said to be a "tabernacle and a heavenly bridegroom coming out of his chamber." The dwelling place of the sun is like a tabernacle or tent because the sun sits in the midst of the constellations. Like a bridegroom coming from a chamber, the sun at dawn comes out of its heavenly abode. Likewise, the Son of

God is the Bridegroom and the Light of the World who dwells in the midst of His people.

God had created the sun to rise from the east for a sign (Gen. 1:14). A sign is given for the purpose of delivering an important message. God has been using His creation to preach the gospel of peace, "Day unto day . . . and night unto night" (Ps. 19:2). For this reason, all unbelievers are without excuse (Rom. 1:20–23) for their rebellion against the Savior of the world (John 4:42). The proclamation of the gospel in the heavenlies "has gone out to all the earth, and their words to the ends of the world" (Rom. 10:18).

ENDNOTES

CHAPTER ONE

1. Tom Pratt, "Falwell: Israel Needs US Support," Tyler, Texas; *Courier-Times-Telegraph*, 6 February 1983.
2. Louis Bahjat Hamada, *God Loves the Arabs, Too* (Nashville: The Hamada Evangelistic Outreach, Inc., 1988), pp. 56–7.
3. Ibid., p. 57.
4. Kenneth Briggs, "Christians and Jews Seek Dialogue," *New York Times*, 11 December 1977.
5. Religious proselytizing in Israel was made illegal in 1978; the maximum sentence for Christian violators is five years imprisonment.
6. "Biblical Right to Israel Affirmed by Begin in Address to Evangelicals," *Religious News Service*, 22 February 1978.
7. Nelson Bell, "Unfolding Destiny," *Christianity Today*, 21 July 1967, p. 1077.
8. William Whiston, *Josephus* (Grand Rapids: Kregel Publications, reprinted, 1980), p. 32.
9. *Wycliffe Bible Commentary* (Chicago: Moody Press, 1974), tenth printing, 31. The interested reader should see the story of Jacob and Esau, Genesis 27:1–46.
10. *The Jewish Encyclopedia*, "Jesus," vol. 7 (New York: Funk & Wagnalls, 1902), p. 170.
11. Ibid., p. 172.
12. *The Universal Jewish Encyclopedia*, ed. by Isaac Landman, "Authority" (New York: Universal Jewish Encyclopedia, Inc., 1939), 634.
13. The Babylonian Talmud (New York: The Rebecca Bennet Publications, Inc., 1959), Aboth 1:1.
14. *The Jewish Encyclopedia*, op. cit., "Authority," p. 337.
15. *Universal Jewish Encyclopedia*, op. cit., "Judaism," p. 235.

16. Ibid., p. 236.
17. Ibid., p. 474.
18. Louis Finkelstein, *The Pharisees* (Philadelphia: The Jewish Publication Society of America, 1966), vol. 2, pp. 780–81.
19. *The Jewish Encyclopedia,* op. cit., "Pharisees," vol. 9, 666.
20. *Wycliffe Bible Commentary*, op. cit., 1002.
21. Ibid., "Jesus," vol. 7, p. 170.
22. The Babylonian Talmud, op. cit., Sanhedrin 43*a*.
23. *The Jewish Encyclopedia*, op. cit., "Balaam," vol. 2, p. 469.
24. Ibid., "Jesus," vol. 7, p. 172.
25. The Babylonian Talmud, op. cit., Gittin 56*b*–57*a*.
26. Grace Halsell, *Prophecy and Politics* (Chicago: Lawrence Hill Books, 1986), p. 12.

CHAPTER TWO

1. Clyde T. Francisco, "The Curse on Canaan," *Christianity Today,* 24 April 1964, pp. 8–10.
2. J. Lloyd, *An Analysis of the First Eleven Chapters of the Book of Genesis* (London: Samuel Bagster and Sons, 1869), p. 111.
3. John Calvin, *Commentaries on the First Book of Moses Called Genesis,* translated by John King, vol. 2 (Edinburgh: The Edinburgh Printing Co., 1847), p. 305.
4. *Biblia Hebraica Stuttgartensia*, ed. by R. Kittel, (Stuttgart: Deutsche Bibelgesellschaft, 1990), p. 13.
5. Lloyd, p. 109.
6. Ibid., p. 110.
7. Francis A. Schaeffer, *Genesis in Space and Time* (Downers Grove, Ill: InterVarsity Press, 1975), p. 149.
8. Arthur C. Custance, *Noah's Three Sons* (Grand Rapids: Zondervan Publishing House, 1975), p. 27.
9. Merrill F. Unger, *Unger's Bible Dictionary* (Chicago: Moody Press, 1973), p. 231.
10. Lloyd, p. 109.
11. C. F. Keil and F. Delitsch, "The Pentateuch," *Commentary on the Old Testament*, vol. 1 (Grand Rapids: Wm. B. Eerdmans, 1973), p. 157.
12. *The Arab World Journal* (New York: vol. 11, no. 3, 1965), p. 54.
13. Leon J. Wood, *A Survey of Israel's History* (Grand Rapids: Zondervan Publishing House, 1976), p. 169.

CHAPTER THREE

1. William Whiston, *Works of Josephus*, vol. 2 (Grand Rapids: Baker Book House, fourteenth printing, 1988), p. 96.

2. Fulcher of Chartres, *A History of Expedition to Jerusalem,* 1095–1127, translated and edited by Frances Rita Ryan (Knoxville: University of Tennessee Press, 1969), p. 66.

3. Louis Bahjat Hamada, *Understanding the Arab World* (Nashville: Thomas Nelson, 1990), p. 112.

4. Norman F. Cantor, *The Meaning of the Middle Ages* (Boston: Allyn and Bacon, Inc., 1973), p. 178.

5. Ibid., p. 180.

6. Bertrand Russell, *A History of Western Philosophy* (New York: Simon and Schuster, 1945), p. 338.

7. Gordon Leff, *Medieval Thought: St Augustine to Ockham* (Harmondsworth, Middlesex, England: Penguin Books, Ltd., 1970), pp. 45–6.

8. Cantor, op. cit., p. 180.

9. Ibid., p. 52.

10. Robert the Monk, *Historia Iheresolimitana,* quoted by August C. Krey, *The First Crusade: The Accounts of Eye-Witnesses and Participants* (Princeton and London: Princeton University Press, 1921), p. 30.

11. Chartres, op. cit., p. 66.

12. *Gesta Francorum,* or *The Deeds of the Franks and the Other Pilgrims to Jerusalem,* translated by Rosalind Hill (London: T. Nelson, 1962), p. 37.

13. Karen Armstrong, *Holy War: The Crusades and Their Impact on Today's World* (New York: Anchor Books, 1991), pp. 56–59.

14. Besides general sources on world history, much of the following information was gleaned from *Arab Historians of the Crusades,* selected and translated to the Italian from the Arabic sources by Francesco Gabrieli, and translated from the Italian to English by E. J. Costello (New York: Anchor Books, 1989); and *Holy War,* Armstrong, op. cit.

15. The Muslims believe prophet Muhammad ascended into heaven from the Dome of the Rock. Nearby, the Mosque of al-Masjid al-Aqsa, where the crusaders showed more barbarity, according to Ibn al-Athir, the Arabian historian.

Chapter Four

1. *Foxe's Book of Martyrs,* edited by Marie Gentert King (Old Tappan, N.J.: Fleming H. Revell, Co.), p. 13.

2. Angelo Di Berardino, *Encyclopedia of the Early Church,* translated from the Italian by Adrian Walford (New York: Oxford University Press, 1992), p. 404.

3. J. G. Davies, *The Early Christian Church* (Grand Rapids, Michigan: Baker Book House, 1978), pp. 143–9.

4. J. B. Lightfoot, *The Apostolic Fathers* (Grand Rapids, Michigan: Baker Book House, 1978), p. 77.

5. Di Berardino, op. cit., p. 404.

6. Lightfoot, op. cit., p. 63.

7. Lightfoot, op. cit., p. 77.

8. Herbert J. Thurston, S. J., and Donald Attwater, *Butler's Lives of the Saints*, vol. 2 (Westminster, Maryland: Christian Classics, Inc., 1981), pp. 88–9.

9. *The Ecclesiastical History of Eusebius Pamphilus* (Grand Rapids, Michigan: Baker Book House, 1991), pp. 143–9.

10. Lightfoot, op. cit., pp. 109–10.

11. *Eusebius*, op. cit., p. 146.

12. *Eusebius*, op. cit., p. 148.

13. Di Berardino, op. cit., pp. 462–3.

14. Thurston, op. cit., pp. 88–9.

15. Thurston, op. cit., pp. 89–90.

CHAPTER FIVE

1. Some of these blessings and retributions were discussed in my two previous books: *God Loves the Arabs, Too* and *Understanding the Arab World.*

2. *Christians and Israel: A Quarterly Publication from Jerusalem*, vol. 4, no. 1, Winter 1994/95, p. 4.

3. *The Interpreter's Bible*, edited by Nolan B. Harmon, vol. 5 (New York: Abingdon Press, 1956), pp. 161–2.

4. Ibid., pp. 161–2.

5. *The Anchor Bible Dictionary*, edited by David Noel Freedman, vol. 2 (New York: Doubleday, 1992), pp. 359–60.

6. Under the Pharaohs, Egypt was divided into Upper and Lower, "the two regions," *ta-tee,* were called "the Southern Region," *ta-res*, and "the Northern Region," *ta-meheet.* There were different crowns for the two regions, that of Upper Egypt being white, and that of Lower Egypt, red; the two together composing the *pschent*—the double crown of Egypt, used after the union of the two kingdoms under Menes. The sovereign had a special title as ruler of each region: of Upper Egypt he was *suten*, "king," and of Lower Egypt, *shebt*, "bee." The two combined formed the common title *suten-shebt.* The initial sign of the former name is a bent reed, which illustrates what seems to have been a proverbial expression in Palestine as to the danger of trusting to the Pharaohs and Egypt. William Smith, *Dictionary of*

the Bible, vol. 1. (Boston: Houghton, Mifflin and Company; 1890), p. 669.

7. Hamada, op. cit., pp. 139–42.

8. The Vulgate is the Old Testament translation from Hebrew to Latin; the Septuagint is the Old Testament translation from Hebrew to Greek.

9. John F. Walvoord, *Jesus Christ Our Lord* (Chicago: Moody Press, 1969), p. 154.

10. *Josephus: Complete Works*, translated by William Whiston (Grand Rapids, Michigan: Kregel Publications, 1981), p. 55.

11. Ibid., pp. 55–6.

12. Erwin W. Lutzer and John F. DeVries, *Satan's Evangelistic Strategy for This New Age* (Wheaton, Illinois: Victor Books, 1989), p. 17.

13. The Arabs are approximately 300 million, and not all of them are Muslims. The Muslims are more than 1.5 billion.

CHAPTER SIX

1. James G. Macqueen, *Babylon* (Frederick A. Praeger Publishers, 1964), p. 174.

2. Alexander Hislop, *The Two Babylons* (Neptune, New Jersey: Loizeaux Brothers, 1959), p. 31.

3. Material summarized from Hislop, *The Two Babylons*.

4. Francis A. Schaeffer, *How Should We Then Live* (Old Tappan, N.J.: Fleming H. Revell Co., 1976), pp. 20–2.

5. A. G. Dickens, *The English Reformation* (New York: Schocken Books, 1974), p. 22.

6. Matthew Spinka, *John Huss* (Princeton, New Jersey: Princeton University Press, 1968), p. 133.

7. Ibid., pp. 137–139.

8. John Dillenberger, *Martin Luther: Selections from His Writings* (Garden City, New York: Anchor Books, 1961), p. 250.

9. Hislop, p. 20.

10. Ibid., p. 105.

11. Dillenberger, pp. 54–55.

12. H. A. Ironside, *Except Ye Repent* (Grand Rapids, Michigan: Zondervan, 1937), p. 7.

13. For a better understanding of the definition of repentance, please consult J. H. Thayer, *Thayer's Greek Lexicon* (Grand Rapids, Michigan: Zondervan, 1962), p. 406.

14. Philo, *Philo I: Loeb Classical Library*, "Legum Allegoria" (Cambridge: Harvard University Press, 1981), pp. 191–95.

15. Whiston, *Josephus,* (1980), p. 25.

16. John of Damascus, *Nicene and Post-Nicene Fathers*, "Exposition of the Orthodox Faith," vol. 3 (Grand Rapids: Wm. B. Eerdmans, 1979); book 2, chap. 9.
17. Whiston, p. 25.
18. William Smith, *Dictionary of the Bible*, vol. 1 (Cambridge: Riverside Press, H. O. Houghton & Co., 1868–70), p. 657.
19. *Aramco World Magazine*, March–April 1980.
20. Hamada, p. 48.
21. Ibid., p. 49.
22. Smith, vol. 1, p. 657.
23. Louis Bahjat Hamada, *God Loves the Arabs, Too* (Nashville: The Hamada Evangelistic Outreach, Inc., 1988), p. 14.
24. Smith, vol. 1, p. 520.
25. Jerome, *Nicene and Post-Nicene Fathers*, "Letters," vol. 6.

CHAPTER SEVEN

1. Philo, pp. 191–95.
2. Whiston, *Josephus*, (1980), p. 25.
3. John of Damascus, book 2, chap. 9.
4. Whiston, p. 25.
5. Smith, vol. 1, p. 657.
6. *Aramco World Magazine*, March–April 1980.
7. Hamada, *Understanding the Arab World,* p. 48.
8. Ibid., p. 49.
9. Smith, vol. 1., p. 657.
10. Louis Bahjat Hamada, *God Loves the Arabs, Too* (Nashville: The Hamada Evangelistic Outreach, Inc., 1988), p. 14.
11. Smith, vol. 1., p. 520.
12. Jerome, *Nicene and Post-Nicene Fathers*, "Letters", vol. 6.
13. Unger, p. 482.
14. Smith, vol. 4, p. 3249.
15. Phillip K. Hitti, *History of the Arabs*, tenth edition (New York: St. Martin's Press, 1970), p. 349.
16. Unger, p. 285.
17. W. F. Albright, *From the Stone Age to Christianity* (Baltimore: Johns Hopkins Press, 1946), p. 6.
18. San Juan de la Cruz, *Vida y Obras de San Juan de la Cruz*, "Cantico Espiritual," (Madrid: La Editorial Catolica, 1955), pp. 1024–5.

ABOUT THE AUTHOR

L ouis Bahjat Hamada was born on October 12, 1928, to an aristocratic Lebanese family in Hawran (biblical Haran), a Southwestern district of Syria, where his father served as prosecutor general under the French mandatory rule. After the untimely death of his parents, Hamada was reared in Lebanon by his grandfather, who was the head of the Druze religion, an outgrowth of the Shiite sect of Islam.

Hamada came to the US in 1953 and was converted to faith in Christ on September 11, 1955. Since then, he has earned a Ph.D. in music education from Florida State University and a master's degree from Dallas Theological Seminary. He has also earned a Doctor of Letters degree (Litt.D.) from Oxford Graduate School and was officially inducted into the Oxford Society of Scholars on October 22, 1994. This was based on his "excellence in research related to problem-solving within the family, community, and church and contributing to knowledge potentially enhancing the spiritual growth of the body of Christ." He has led Bible conferences and revivals across North America and abroad and has conducted seminars at various Bible colleges and universities.

Dr. Hamada is an ordained minister of the gospel of Christ and a noted Bible teacher and a recognized authority on Semitic Arabs and Muslim evangelization. He is the founder of a faith ministry: The Hamada Evangelistic Outreach, Inc.

Hamada's international ministry of preaching and teaching has been used to help spread the good news of Jesus Christ during these tumultuous days. Grieved over unfortunate misconceptions and misconstrued interpretations of biblical truths that many Christians have adopted concerning the Arabs and Muslims, Dr. Hamada has been given the ability to clarify these interpretations in a clear and concise manner.

His faith in Christ as Lord and Savior is undergirded by a staunch, unswerving commitment to the inerrant, plenary inspiration of the written Word of God.

Dr. Hamada may be contacted for speaking engagements at the following address:

Dr. Louis Hamada
PO Box 3333
Jackson, TN 38303
ph: (901) 668-8350
fax: (901) 668-7102
e-mail: lhamada@iname.com

To order additional copies of

Is the Holy Land Holy?

send $11.99* plus $4.95 shipping and handling to

Books, Etc.
PO Box 1406
Mukilteo, WA 98275

or have your credit card ready and call

(800) 917-BOOK

*Quantity discounts available